Simple Spells
for Hearth and Home

Simple Spells
for Hearth and Home

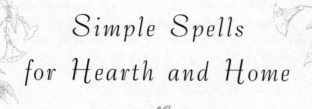

Ancient Practices
for Creating Harmony,
Peace, and Abundance

Barrie Dolnick

Harmony Books
New York

Published by Harmony Books, 201 East 50th Street, New York, New York 10022.
Member of the Crown Publishing Group.
Random House, Inc. New York, Toronto, London, Sydney, Auckland
www.randomhouse.com
Harmony Books is a registered trademark and Harmony Books colophon is a trademark of Random House, Inc.
Printed in the United States of America

Design by Donna Sinisgalli

Library of Congress Cataloging-in-Publication Data
Dolnick, Barrie.
Simple spells for hearth and home : ancient practices for creating harmony, peace, and abundance / Barrie Dolnick.
1. Magic. 2. Home—Miscellanea. I. Title.
BF1623.H67D65   2000
133.4'4—dc21   99-34145
CIP

ISBN 0-609-60427-9
10 9 8 7 6 5 4 3 2 1
First Edition

for

Elisabeth Lee Johanna

Acknowledgments

This book was written with the gentle reassurance and guidance of my agent, Emma Sweeney, and warm support and energy from my editor, Shaye Areheart.

I am most grateful to the people who have shared the magic of their homes and occasions with me: Cheryl Callan and Ed Milian, Julia Condon, Alexandra and James Brown, Ilene Chaiken and Miggi Hood, Sheila and Tony Davidson, Nancy Mayers and Bob Furnds, Tricia and Tim McCann, Halo and Friedel Miesenboeck, Cynthia Purmort and Mary Ann LaBue, Mary Lou and Joe Quinlan, Susan Strong, Cheryl Kraus and Boris Zemelman.

I thank my sisters for their humor and sarcasm, my mother for the hearth and home of my youth, Suzie for keeping this home smooth and sane, and Mitch Popovic for his friendship and help.

I most especially thank my husband, Gero, for his love, support, and unquantifiable faith in my work and for giving me the opportunity to explore Vesta's magic in our own hearth and home.

And to 4909 North Ardmore Avenue, the home that still holds a piece of my heart.

Contents

Preface   *17*

Introduction   *19*

O N E

Your Magical Home   35

T W O

Enchantments for Every Room   53

T H R E E

General Atmosphere Enhancers   77

F O U R

Spells for Holidays and Special Occasions   99

F I V E

Nature's Harmony in Your Home   127

S I X

Spells for Selling and Saying Good-Bye   155

Afterword   *169*

Index   *171*

We need not power or splendor;

Wide hall or lordly dome;

The good, the true, the tender,

These form the wealth of home.

SARAH JOSEPHA HALE

Simple Spells
for Hearth and Home

Preface

I've never considered myself a homebody, and until recently I didn't have a great deal of interest in what a home really stands for or gives to me. In the past, my books tracked my own life experience: With *Simple Spells for Love* I met my husband and got married; with *Simple Spells for Success* I became a solid author and speaker and produced two more books. Now, with *Simple Spells for Hearth and Home,* I am truly living the nature and magic of establishing a home where my family and I can live in harmony.

Being a homemaker is not easy. Creating a healthy, secure, supportive environment takes a great deal of consideration and, frankly, a lot of life force. You are weaving your energy into your physical environment, and supposedly getting rest, comfort, a respite from the outer world in return. And if you happen to be raising a family on top of this, you're really living on the edge.

I was reminded why I was writing *Simple Spells for Hearth and Home* during a cozy afternoon in the kitchen of our close friends Cindy and Mary Ann. Their home is filled with comfortable furniture, photographs of their extensive families, lots of collectibles, art, and objects that make each room interesting and engaging. There we were, sitting in their large country kitchen, drinking coffee and catching up on life, when Cindy wondered why we hadn't moved to the living room.

"We just got those great couches to make the living room more comfortable, but here we are, still sitting around the kitchen table."

She had a point. The living room, where we'd sat after dinner the previous evening, was very comfortable and attractive, but we still sat during the day on hard wooden chairs at a rectory table without even thinking about it. Why?

The hearth. I'm convinced it's our friend Vesta, the goddess of the hearth, who keeps us close to her ancient fire. Vesta is also Hestia, from ancient Greece, keeper of the flame, the hearth fire that meant heat, cooking, cleaning for the generations before us. People often slept, ate, and lived in one room. The fire in their hearth was their assurance that they would not freeze or starve.

We carry the tradition of the hearth into our homes today. Many kitchens now open onto the living room or playroom, and most of us treasure that time spent at the kitchen table. But you can also carry this magical feeling into other rooms in the house so that they, too, can be special spaces for you and your family.

Simple Spells for Hearth and Home is a guide for bringing the best "living" energy into your home so that you can recharge, rest, and grow in an atmosphere that feeds you and your family best.

Introduction

Home is where the heart is. Old-fashioned? Definitely. Trite—but true. Coming home from a long and strenuous workday, you want to relax in the best possible environment. Your home is your recharger—the place you come to to find your center, your peace, to refuel your energy. If you're bringing a new baby into the world, you'll want to make sure that your home is supportive and loving. If you're celebrating family events or holidays, or just passing each day as best you can, your home is your center, your solitude, your sanctuary. A new coat of paint or a little aluminum siding can help keep it standing, but the real life of the place comes from you.

Whether your taste is romantic or minimal, Bauhaus or Renaissance, first-class antiques or recycled flea market, your environment is infused with energy—a psychic, emotional, and passionate combination of life force that you create. You can feel the atmosphere of a house at its threshold. The environment speaks to you.

Every piece of furniture, every picture, carpet, blanket, or trinket—everything in your home holds some kind of energy that contributes to its atmosphere. You've chosen to weave your own energetic quilt in your unique mix of decor.

Every person, animal, plant, even insect leaves impressions of emotional and psychic energy in your home. Emotions are very powerful atmospheric imprints; anger can destroy a peaceful decor just as joy can color a barren room. Emotional atmosphere is often palpable when you visit someone's house. More subtle is the psychic energy of a place; this will leave you with an underlying mood. For instance, if a room is psychically shut down or dimmed, you could end up feeling tired or drained. You've probably felt this already in an office or waiting room—those are notoriously dead spaces. Both emotional and psychic energy can color your entire experience in a place and even be carried with you when you leave. Your home is one place where you can control emotional and psychic atmosphere—and even manipulate it to suit your needs.

This begs the question: What is your household saying about you, and how are you affecting others already?

You create the environment in which you live—consciously or unconsciously.

Is your home powerful, supportive, and pleasant? Welcoming or off-putting? Safe or threatening?

The most basic purpose of your home is to shelter you from the elements of nature and from strangers. It is truly a sacred place, the apex of your power to protect and thrive.

Personally, I never thought about how I felt inside my home. It wasn't until I started to study spells and learn about psychic energy that I realized how every square inch of my house made some contribution to my well-being—or not. I reluctantly admit that I once lived in a very nonsupportive environment—harsh white walls, minimal, "practical" furniture, and few decorative touches. No wonder I always looked for reasons to get out of the house. Once I learned about infusing an environment with supportive and life-enhancing energy, though, that inhospitable place became my safe haven.

Simple Spells for Hearth and Home will guide you through some easy processes to create the atmosphere and energy that make your home unique, loving, and safe. This book offers you advice for creating an environment that nurtures and protects the soul; you will learn how to conjure atmospheres, clear away negative energy, establish protection and emotional support, even ease tension. This isn't about furniture placement or lines and design—it's about weaving your intention, passion, and very nature into your home to help you live a healthy and happy life.

A WORD ON FENG SHUI

Feng shui, the Chinese method of aligning a household with "chi," or the earth's natural energy, has become quite popular in recent years. The premise of feng shui is that there are angles, directions, and placements within your household that can contribute positively to your life force, health, and wealth.

Simple Spells for Hearth and Home is perfectly compatible with feng shui and other methods of geomancy, but here's the difference: Rather than work with the earth's chi energy, these simple spells allow you to shift the atmosphere of your household with your own heart and soul. Your power, intention, and connection are used to conjure the end results.

THE MAGIC OF YOU

You may be just getting started in the world of spells and magic. It's an amazing world full of untapped potential and possibilities. You may not even know that you're already creating magic—every day. You're already unconsciously influencing your environment and shifting reality just by the kind of plants you have (or don't have), the colors you choose, the scent you use, the emotions you feel or deny. You are, by nature, already a magician. Just wait until you really know what you're doing—and enjoy the results.

WHAT IS A SPELL?

For those of you who have read *Simple Spells for Love* or *Simple Spells for Success,* this will sound familiar. To the best of my knowledge and experience, *a spell is an organized wish that carries with it the power to manifest a desire.*

A spell is a ritual—a process we often do without thinking. For instance, celebrating a birthday, we light candles on a cake, make a wish, and enjoy the blessings of our friends and family—that's a spell. A housewarming, too, is a spell, one during which people come to bless the new dwelling, share good wishes, and raise a glass to the hosts' happy and healthy future. You can find spells everywhere—in religious rites, at parties, even just in the steps you take to get ready to go out for an evening.

ELEMENTAL MAGIC

The basis of spell-casting comes in part from a tradition called elemental magic, an ancient practice that paid homage to the four basic elements of life: fire, earth, air, and water. Prior to Judeo-Christian culture, rituals often included representation of each element, and if you look around your current house of worship, you'll still find them. Fire is represented by candles and/or an eternal flame. Earth is often plentiful in the form of flowers, books, or icons. Air can be seen in both incense and prayer that's spoken aloud. Water is often found in a cup of wine or represented by a bowl or chalice.

A brief look at each of these elements may help you understand their potency when it comes to your spells.

Fire is the first element and is commonly identified with two properties: combustion and illumination. In elemental magic, fire is more complex. Combustion produces heat—passion, anger, initiative, and transformation. Illumination certainly sheds light, but it also pioneers new territory, explores and leads. It's no accident that fire is our first element—we need it for impetus and fuel. The term *hearth* is connected to the fire element in the old saying "Keep the home fire burning." Fire is essential to home life.

Earth is the element most often connected with the home, since it rules material reality. Earth is what your house is built on and made from—everything organic and physical is a symbol of earth. Earth, therefore, represents security, luxury, comfort, and tactile pleasures.

Air, the third element, is primarily intellectual. The mind, thoughts, and communication are air-ruled and are subject to the air qualities of clarity, sharpness, and fog. Air is important for atmospheric spells and for clearing negativity.

The fourth element, water, takes on many dimensions. Water represents emotions, feelings, imagination, and intuition. Water can be still and hard (ice), smooth and flowing (liquid), and foggy and thick (steam). Take these physical forms of water and consider how they might feel if they were emotions, or emotional atmosphere. The water element in your atmosphere isn't always obvious, but it is very much present and is largely responsible for the mood you create.

Representation of the elements is used not just for symbolism, but for the energy each element brings to your spell. Elemental magic is performed with a specific purpose in mind, and each object you use will contain or represent a power you need in order to conjure the result you're after. For example, a candle may be orange or yellow to bring in energy or vitality, or pink or blue to add calmness or heart's ease. The plant or flowers you choose often have ancient associations of healing powers or magnetism. Certainly the words you say are directed to the purpose; water is the only element that is usually in its basic form.

Bringing together the four elements for ritual with a specific purpose is the very core of elemental magic.

WHAT ARE SPELLS FOR HEARTH AND HOME?

The Magic of Vesta

Casting spells for your household is not intended to transform your home into the gingerbread house from the story of Hansel and Gretel (and you may remember a nasty old witch lived there, which is definitely not where I'm taking you). Spells for hearth and home are very old and easily traced back to ancient Greece and Rome. The Greeks worshiped Hestia, goddess of the hearth, the all-important source for heat and cooking. Romans adopted Hestia and renamed her Vesta, the goddess of hearth and home. Vesta was the first god invoked at all festivals, as a sign of respect for her importance. Every so often you'll see Vesta's name in these spells, which I've done to give her the proper respect and acknowledgment. She has been around in one form or another longer than any of us.

In case you're concerned that doing these spells will make you a reborn pagan, not to worry. Spells for hearth and home are acknowledgments, celebrations, and remedies that can incorporate your current religious (or nonreligious) affiliation.

Spells for hearth and home can help you create the most productive and supportive environment for you and your family by asking the universe to help.

Spells are not about control or casting your power over someone, some room, or some event. Instead, spells focus on making the best experience possible for all those involved. These spells are for the "greater good," which means you can't decide what's best for everyone—the universe (god) will do that for you.

You may be wondering how these spells work. There is no right answer to explain how your own magic makes things happen, but it is most likely through a combination of forces. Your energy, the energy provided by the things around you, and the energy of the universe will team up to intersect and manifest the best of all possible outcomes. You won't see it happen, and it won't be what you expect—that's the fun of performing simple spells. The universe is full of surprises, and your imagination is not nearly as creative as the cosmos. Spells for hearth and home enable you to keep a constant connection going with the universe so that you can consciously maximize all of your efforts.

Celebrations and blessings can also be enhanced by using simple spells. Just connecting to the elements or performing a small rite with intention can lead to a stronger experience and a more enduring memory.

MAGIC AND OBJECTIVITY

In all spells and magic, the outcome is a manifestation of all you put into it. You will be very conscious of most of your spell ingredients, but you may add a few emotional components that may tinge the mix. It isn't appropriate to cast a spell unless you are as open, neutral, and objective as you can be. Hidden anger, sadness, anxiety—all negative or "sticky" emotions may taint the spell and hence its outcome.

My client Buffy found this out the hard way. She wanted to sell her house quickly and was quite anxious about making it all "happen" on her terms. She cast a spell for a quick sale within her asking-price range, but she did so with an edge in her emotional energy. She even recalls that she clenched her hands during her spell and that she ended it more forcefully than she had intended. As with most spells, her efforts paid off, but her energy echoed back to her. The buyer was just as anxious to complete the deal as Buffy had been to sell, and their anxiety levels played off of each other. The deal went through, but it was accompanied by many headaches and phone calls that didn't need to happen.

When you cast your spells and energize your atmospheres, do so with as much clarity as possible. It isn't always simple to feel relaxed and easy about something you badly want to happen, but if you can find a way to do a spell with a minimum of "sticky" emotions, you'll have a better result.

SPELL REQUIREMENTS:
BELIEF, INTENTION, ALLOWING

Related to the topic of objectivity is my recipe for your part in performing a spell. You need to possess three qualities for your spells to work: belief, intention, and allowing.

Belief
Belief is an issue for most people—particularly skeptics! We're all prone to a little disbelief and questioning when it comes to magic. It's natural.

You don't need to be childlike and, as in the story of Peter Pan, clap hard to show you believe in magic. You simply need to have a small part of yourself accept that magic is possible. Even staying with "I don't know if it works, but I'll give it a try" is good enough. Nothing shuts down magic faster than a closed mind and heart.

Belief is very personal and probably very private for most. When interviewed by the press, I'm often asked, "Do you really believe in this stuff?"

I always answer, with a sly smile, "Yes." I've seen spells work so often now that I'd be a fool to say otherwise—but that doesn't mean I believe everything. You, too, can maintain some healthy skepticism while you perform your magic—just allow some space for believing in it, too.

Intention

The second quality you must possess is intention. This is the energy that makes up your purpose or direction. Intention is the real personal power behind a spell. You intend to make a place safe, loving, secure. You intend to give a pleasurable evening to your company. You intend to make an atmosphere healing and gentle for all who may need it.

The more specific your intention, the more clear your outcome. At the same time, though, you need to beware of a deviant of "good intention," which is the energy of your will getting in the way. Willful energy is too strong and can squash the magic right out of a spell.

My client Jerry's intention was to throw an exceptional anniversary party for his parents. He wanted to create a great event and a lasting memory, and (unconsciously) he wanted to show his parents how much he would do for them. He planned to use his home, a spacious ranch house, for the party, and before planning the details, Jerry performed a spell to create the right mix of fun, sentiment, and entertainment.

While Jerry did undertake an enormous effort in doing the cooking, planning the guest list, devising the decorations, and even hiring a band, his will got in his way. He didn't consult or listen to his parents, who wanted a small family gathering—nor did he heed the appeals of his wife and children, who wanted to take part in the preparations. Jerry's willfulness blocked out the potential to create the kind of intimacy his parents wanted because he didn't listen to them—or to the universe gently nudging him to shift his ideas. Unfortunately, Jerry didn't enjoy himself as much as he thought he would; his family wasn't responding as warmly as he had expected, and he was exhausted by his single-handed efforts, which had worked against the greater good.

Willfulness is hard to remove from your spells, so pay attention to the force and control you feel over the outcome. Once you learn to trust that the universe knows better than you, you won't feel the need to be so hands-on.

Allowing

Related to intention is allowing, the hands-*off* process of letting the spell happen. Intention gives your spell its basic purpose, and allowing is the energy that helps transform your purpose into reality. Allowing is really hard; you are supposed to trust the universe and let your magic happen in its own time.

Allowing is particularly difficult when you want something to happen on your own timetable. Trust me, the universe doesn't work on standard or daylight savings time—it works on what I like to refer to as Cosmic Time. In Cosmic Time, there isn't a calendar or a due date, there's only "when it's right." When you're trying to sell a house or find one, Cosmic Time isn't easy to trust, but it will always work in your favor.

I myself had to trust the big Cosmic clock just recently. I was about to give birth to our daughter, and my husband and I were living in a one-bedroom apartment in Manhattan at a time when the real-estate market was very tight and apartments were expensive. I waited until the right time to cast my spell—for "the right place for the three of us to live." By the time I had the baby, no apartment was in sight. Our newborn daughter slept in our bedroom in a cozy nook we created by taking the doors off of our walk-in closet, but by the time she was four months old, we wanted to give her a real room of her own and reclaim ours—but still no apartment in sight. I figured my spell didn't work (I blamed my willful hormones), and I tried to figure out how to chop up our apartment to make a baby's room. But then, as soon as I gave up waiting for the spell to work, it did. Our landlord called and asked us if we wanted to move upstairs into a two-bedroom with a park view, and we accepted gratefully.

I needed to let the spell work on its own time, which is a lesson that I still need to learn even after my many years of spell-casting.

Not everyone has to give up on their spell to allow it to happen, though. All you need to do is trust that the universe is listening to you and that your prayer will be answered. Find a state of assurance with room for mystery and you've found the state of allowing.

PRIMARY SPELLS

Since magic is so personal and creative, it is important and empowering to understand how to make up your own spells. Throughout this book I provide you with what I call primary spells, fundamental spells that work on the intention stated, and also some secondary or supporting spells that can contribute more facets to your work. Once you get the hang of these spells, you'll be able to conjure up your own.

A primary spell is a great foundation for the general purpose at hand. For instance, you may want to sell your home; there is a basic spell for getting this energy going. Or you may be interested in establishing the sensation of playfulness and unity in your family room—there is also a primary spell for this. However, there are likely to be other things you'll want to conjure in these rooms, too, and this is where the supporting spells come in. Supporting spells are overlays of magic on the primary spell.

Atmospheres, one form of supporting spell, can be created very quickly (with practice, that is) and can be used for almost every part of the day. There's nothing like a cozy Sunday morning or, conversely, a festive Saturday night atmosphere—and you're probably already creating those well. You'll find atmospheric manipulations are particularly useful when you need to change your indoor climate. Take the gloom out of a rainy day; shift the tension of waiting for something to happen—there are many uses for atmospheric shifts. Your basic family room can be converted from its warm and familial atmosphere to a somber, magical space for spell work. You're already doing some kind of atmospheric spell work just by lighting candles or adding flowers to a room—supporting spells can just add a little more zip to your zap.

HOW TO FIND WHAT YOU NEED: SPELL INGREDIENTS

As I've ensured in the title of this book, *Simple Spells for Hearth and Home,* I do my best to keep these spell ingredients simple and accessible. Since the publication of my first spell book, *Simple Spells for Love,* there has been a veritable explosion of spell ingredients in the marketplace. You should have no trouble finding candles in different colors—practically every catalog and home store has a great selection. Nor should you have any problem finding scents—you can use candles, potpourri, or bath oils to help you in the few instances you'll need a fragrance. When you need herbs, you can start by looking in your spice cabinet (cinnamon is a favorite in spell-casting) and, if necessary, your garden or a health-food store. There will be no need, I hope, for you to go to great lengths to find an ingredient, and if you can't find it, skip it. Spells work most powerfully from your intention, not your ability to shop.

The great thing about spells for the home is that they are deeply personal. Most often your spell ingredients will consist of things that you already own. Don't worry about how special, sacred, or spiritual the source for your spell ingredients is. Of course, it doesn't hurt to harvest herbs or flowers from your own blessed garden, but I don't demand it. Gathering your spell ingredients is done primarily with your heart, and even if you're dumping out lavender from an old sachet in your underwear drawer (I've done this), it's perfectly good for a spell.

THE ESSENTIALS OF SPELL TIMING

However relaxed you can be about spell ingredients, be less so with spell timing. There are important times of the month and even the year for doing some spells, and I insist that you respect this if you want good results.

It's important that you understand that magic is not linear or rational, which can help take the "Why?" out of the equation. Magic happens in the realm of mystery, the unseen and unknown. Therefore spells are best cast at night, or at least after sundown, when the growing darkness allows your magic to work its best. For those of you who need a rational explanation for why this is, think about casting a spell in the bright light of day. Asking for a blessing or a heartfelt desire is tough when you've got physical reality staring you in the face, sending a message to your unconscious that you're being silly or what you want isn't possible. It's much easier to dream in the dark and to join with the cosmos to create what you thought was improbable or impossible.

The Moon

There are times when the moon phase is going to be important to your efforts. The waxing moon, or the process of the moon growing from new to full, is for spells that need the energy of growing or increasing. We'll use the waxing moon for planting, looking for a new home, and growing energy. The waning moon, or the two-week phase when the moon shrinks from full to new, is best for cleansing, diminishing, and selling spells. Look in your newspaper to see the dates of the new moon, the first quarter, and the full moon—these are the two weeks of the waxing moon. From the full moon through the third quarter and until the new moon is a waning moon.

> ✿ Be cautious if you use the evenings of the new
> moon or the full moon for spells; these are nights of
> powerful magic and can produce strong results.

The moon is the planet that rules the unconscious. When you work with the moon's cycles, you link the flow of your personal psychic energy to the tidal forces and earth energy. Farmers have planted by the moon phases for thousands of years. Messing with moon magic is not a good idea.

Growing up in Wisconsin, I was privileged to have attended full-moon parties thrown by a blacksmith in a small town. Those were awesome gatherings. The moon worked its magic and people came from miles around to have a great and often unpredictable experience. Lunacy prevailed.

Planetary Hours and Days

Spell timing also incorporates the days of the week and even the hours of each day. I am less concerned about your accuracy here, particularly with the hours of the day. It's not always easy to perform a spell on the right day at the right time. Whenever possible, get it right, since it adds to the power of your spell. If you can't, though, don't worry; you won't forfeit your outcome.

Every day of the week has a planetary ruler. It's obvious in some names, like Monday, which is ruled by the moon, or Sunday, by the sun. However, since it isn't obvious for every day, I've provided a list with days, ruling planets, and the qualities or topics that are emphasized on that day. You'll eventually use it to help you when you want to design your own spells or schedule an event.

Day	Ruling Planet	Topic/Qualities
Monday	Moon	Home, emotional concerns, nurturing
Tuesday	Mars	Fire, initiation, problem solving, aggression
Wednesday	Mercury	Communication, phones, TVs, radios, conversation, nervous energy
Thursday	Jupiter	Expansion, moving, open houses, adventures and risks
Friday	Venus	Pleasure, luxury, entertainment, decorative efforts
Saturday	Saturn	Hard work, structures, limitation, foundations
Sunday	Sun	Healing, families, blessings

Each day, too, has what are called planetary hours, meaning that every hour after sunset is ruled by a certain planet. In some cases these hours can add a great deal of power to your spell, and at other times they aren't as vital. Use them when and if you can only when appropriate. You'll see them in spells like the following, which start with a specific reference to the day and hour: "On a Monday during a waxing moon and in the third hour after sunset…" This indicates the use of a planetary hour, but given the constraints of your schedule and bedtime, it's not always possible to heed this direction.

THESE SPELLS WORK

They work—they really do. Time and time again I've witnessed spells become reality in the most unexpected and clever ways. I've seen my clients transform their love lives, their work, and their homes from dullness into vibrancy.

I can't offer a firm explanation for how spells work, but it seems that they somehow transport your prayers and wishes into a realm where anything can happen. It just takes a leap of faith on your part to ask for what you want. When you get it, make sure you say thanks, and enjoy your blessings.

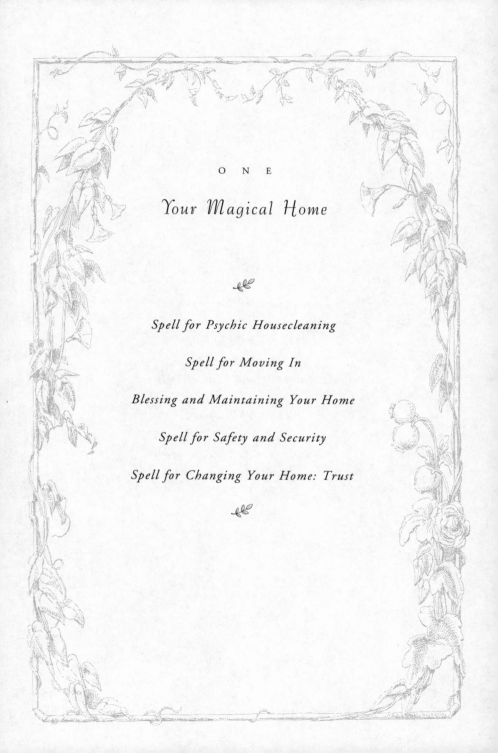

O N E

Your Magical Home

Spell for Psychic Housecleaning

Spell for Moving In

Blessing and Maintaining Your Home

Spell for Safety and Security

Spell for Changing Your Home: Trust

Spell Basics

≈

Time of month: Waxing moon

Day of week: Monday

Time of day: Second hour after sunset

Color: White, green

Flower: Carnations or roses

Herb: Basil

Whether you live in a mansion, apartment, or mobile home, your living space took on a certain amount of energy when it was constructed. The energy of intention that was used in building your house is as important as the building materials. Once in a while you'll find homes that have enormously supportive energy, such as those built with community effort and intention, the result of a house-raising, for example, still seen today in certain rural areas, or in the efforts of Habitat for Humanity. These homes have special, gentle psychic energy and stability from the spirit of their builders. Conversely, some homes are built through an "assembly line," as in prefab buildings or developments where every house looks the same. These homes usually are low on supportive psychic power, since they are replicated over and over again, weakening each home's natural strength of character and identity, and are built often with the intention of profit-making rather than shelter-providing. More typical, though, are homes and apartments that fall somewhere in the middle. These are constructed by "anonymous" workers who build houses or buildings for a living. These structures may have some individual personality and are usually made with the right intention, but will always benefit from a little more spell-casting to make the most of what they've got.

YOUR HOME IS A FAMILY MEMBER

Your home is almost like a live member of your family, and you can consider its birth to have been the moment the lease was made valid or the title was taken. Your home progresses through its life while you evolve through yours.

You can feel a home's life and personality if you pay attention to it. When a house is new, you'll sense an atmosphere of expectancy, spaciousness; at other times it's barren of energy and it makes you want to leave. When a dwelling is vibrant with life, it seems as if there's always an emotional residue in its air—warmth or companionship even when there's no one home, or vague echoes of voices or emotions. I once walked into a house just after the whole family had left for church, and I could swear that the place was filled with chattering kids playing, and people cooking and talking, but no one was there. A household's energy diminishes when its inhabitants are rarely there or slowly move out—"the empty nest" reflects a very real energetic decline in psychic and emotional energy. The stillness or quietness of this kind of atmosphere can be calming and soothing or lonely and detached.

You can keep your home's energy flowing and positive, healing and comforting, no matter what life cycle you're experiencing, but to do this, you have to do a little psychic housecleaning. If you're just moving into a place, you should "clean the house" before the furniture goes in. Before you fill up your space with your energy, clean out what may have been left behind by the last tenants, the painters, the builders, or even the real-estate agents. In spell-casting, I almost always advise a cleansing first.

PSYCHIC HOUSECLEANING

You will need to clean your house psychically more than once, so get used to this idea. The principle of this cleaning is to neutralize any negativity or toxicity that may have been left behind, and to clear out other people's imprints if they are not compatible with yours.

A house is typically imprinted with the energy of its former tenants, particularly if they've lived there a long time. We moved into an apartment that had been totally renovated before we got there, but I still cleared its atmosphere of energy from the prior tenant, a lovely woman who died from liver cancer. I wasn't worried about her ghost or any kind of illness we might be exposed to, but I was concerned about the air of sadness, pain, or decline that she might have felt in her last days. We were moving in with our five-month-old daughter, hoping to establish a happy, healthy, and growing household—a clearing seemed in order.

Even guests or temporary help can imprint their energy on your home's atmosphere. Although it may not be strong enough to affect you overtly, your home could harbor some residual emotion or attitude that just isn't yours. For example, you might feel someone's anger or discomfort after they're gone.

The Clearing Process

A psychic housecleaning or clearing is very simple to perform. I recommend using the Native American technique called "smudging," passing smoldering dried sagebrush around your rooms, to clear away negative energy. Sage has been historically used for cleansing psychically hostile or negative vibrations and also for exorcisms, but you don't have to have large-scale negativity in order to use it—it's an all-purpose cleaner. I often clear spaces before performing spells or conjuring atmospheres just to make sure I'm starting off on clear ground. You'll find a few different clearing rituals in this book, but the most basic form of clearing is explained in this chapter.

You should know that psychic housecleaning is not subtle. Sagebrush has a very strong odor (some say like cannabis), so be aware that your psychic housecleaning will be obvious to anyone around.

A Word on Clearing Poltergeists and Hauntings

Ever since the book and movie about a possessed house in Amityville, Long Island, the media has relished stories of hauntings and unexplained events, attributed to poltergeists (meaning "noise-making" spirits in German) and ghosts. I'm not about to tell you that they don't exist, because they do, but they are fairly rare and often shy. Aggressive hauntings are not something you'd come across easily, nor would you move into a place that has that kind of hostility—you'd pick up that kind of negative energy just viewing the house, and you'd probably not want to return.

I do have personal experience with some menacing demons, and quite a few of my clients and friends have had their own run-ins with nonphysical energies. There is one lesson we have all learned: Just because you can't see them doesn't mean they're more powerful. Actually, the more afraid you are, the more power you give them. Start laughing at a poltergeist and it won't get much satisfaction (as a matter of fact, while I'm writing this, one of my unseen companions has pushed over a shopping bag—I think it's taking issue with this opinion!).

I don't think I could explain what all of these phenomena are, but I do know that there are a lot of different kinds. One common "ghost" is just a clump of energy that can make you feel a dark presence. This kind of "phantom" is intense emotional energy that has gathered in places where something dramatic has happened or there's been sadness, suicide, or trauma. If you perceive a shift in your mood from ease to malaise, or from energetic to sluggish, you may be under siege by this kind of energy. Smudging is important because the sagebrush will keep you fairly protected. Clear yourself with smudge, too, or take a bath or shower, or leave the room for some fresh air. Really strong negative emotional energy is hard to shake off without a shift in climate.

There are real poltergeists, too, which "inhabit" some part of your household or an appliance. I swear I had one behind my refrigerator in our last home. Like most poltergeists, it could summon up enough energy to push things around—plates or platters went flying, sometimes lightbulbs blew out. Poltergeists are not that threatening or destructive, as movies would make you think. They just seem to be bursts of energy that repeatedly occur in the same place in your house and periodically make your home less peaceful. Unless you're really troubled by it, make this little mischief-maker into an eccentric household member and enjoy the occasional spontaneous event—and don't keep breakable things nearby.

Ghosts do exist also and can be very interesting if you get to know them. I am not fortunate enough to have the facility for seeing or communicating with them, but I understand it can be a bit unnerving at first. Ghosts are usually people who have died but have not "passed on" into the next realm. Often they prefer to stay connected to our physical reality, but sometimes they don't know they're dead or they're trying to finish something that didn't get done. It isn't very common to have a nasty ghost around, but if you do, your best bet is to consult a shaman or skilled realm worker who can help you calm the spirit down.

There are, of course, cases of paranormal events that I haven't mentioned or described. The best course of action is always to clear, ask aloud that the spirit or energy leave or at least behave, and try not to be afraid.

PSYCHIC START-UPS: MOVING IN

Once you've cleared the ground of your new place, you can move in with your own energy. When you move into a new space, you are initiating a relationship with it, in a way bonding with the physical energy of your dwelling.

There are many traditions surrounding a new home, like the one portrayed in *It's a Wonderful Life,* where bread is offered so the house may never know hunger, salt is given so that life may always have flavor, and wine is offered as a symbol of prosperity and joy. My father planted a tree when he bought his first house, another ritual to signify growing life and stability.

The purpose of performing a ritual when you first move into your home is to "hook up" to the cosmic force and begin to live in the fullest, most conscious way. Remember, you're hooking up your phone lines, your cable TV, your water and electricity. This is just another one of those start-ups.

Performing a blessing on your household serves a similar purpose, so even if you're past the moving-in point, you can still initiate the energy.

SAFETY AND SECURITY

The *American Heritage Dictionary* defines *security* as "freedom from risk or danger; safety," but security in the physical world is an illusion; there's no such thing as freedom from risk in everyday life. You can get into trouble if you think that your home is impenetrable because you have a great alarm system, the latest in surveillance, and impeccable protection from health hazards or accidents—you could develop a false sense of security. It's true you can reduce the risk of insecurity to a certain extent, but you can't keep bad things from happening altogether.

Trying to set up an entirely secure household will only make its inhabitants feel insecure.

If you devote a lot of energy to developing a fortress on the outside and a completely antibacterial environment on the inside, you'll feed fear to your household. Sure, use a water or air filter if you want to—and install an alarm system if you choose—but don't get carried away with it, or you risk jeopardizing both your atmosphere and your inner peace. Your attention to preventative measures is fine, but defensive behavior can backfire and make your household feel as if there is danger in everything.

Where is real security? It's within you and the members of your household. Real security is about how you and your family face what life presents, good, bad, or indifferent. Inner security gives you a strength and base that make your life much more agreeable and your household more life-supportive. Spells can increase your feeling of security and inner peace—and more important, they can add spiritual protection.

SPIRITUAL PROTECTION

Through spells, you can summon up energy that can act as a divine security system. Ask for your home to be protected and supportive, and the universe will do what it can to help you along. As spells go, conjuring security and safety leads to effective but often less tangible results.

My client Susanne did the spell for safety and security when she heard about burglaries in her neighborhood. She had an alarm system in her home, but so had those who had been burglarized. Susanne asked the universe to help protect her household from loss and danger, and so far she hasn't been hit.

Another client, Morgan, was worried about his kids getting into accidents. He had been a particularly accident-prone child himself and knew the many dangers that lurked in a household. He performed a spell to ask for special protection for little ones playing in his house and garden, so even when he found his twelve-year-old son on the roof of the garage, no one got hurt—unless you count a verbal lashing.

Spells for protection work in ways you don't notice because when they do work, life continues as usual and you don't have to live in constant fear of "what might happen."

When a spell for protection works, your household will feel calm and solid even when people are not. Protection, security, and safety will be felt in the aura and atmosphere your home emits.

CHANGES IN THE HOME

Making changes or adding on to your home can be very stressful. What you want to accomplish may seem conceptually easy but practically fraught with details and expense. You will want to make the right decisions from the beginning because you'll be living with them for a long time.

My wise friend Trish implemented a makeover for her home that required rebuilding all but one room. Her investment of time, energy, and money was enormous, and her results were worth it: on time, within budget, and exactly to her specifications. Her secret? Trust.

In making a change to your home, you will need to trust on many levels, which includes trusting your decisions and your builder. Spells can help you through those tough-to-trust issues. When you're confronted with four estimates, for example, all of which look alike, a spell can ease you toward the right selection. When you have to choose a light fixture at the last minute, your spell will allow you to trust your gut decision and to make that choice without fear. This may sound trivial to you now, but talk to someone in the middle of rebuilding or adding on to their home and they'll tell you that their trust and judgment is constantly challenged.

Adding on to or remodeling your home will of course change its energetic makeup, and you'll want to ensure that whoever you choose to do the work will contribute integrity and quality. Word-of-mouth recommendations are usually the best way to find this important person, but if you don't have any, you can ask the universe to help. Follow your instincts, listen not just with your ears or your budget, and go with the person who feels right, even if it's the more expensive option.

Lydia, one of my associates, remodeled her apartment and suffered through delays at the hands of a builder she hadn't really wanted to use. Her husband had persuaded her to go with someone who was recommended to them and who was cheaper than her choice, but he was very slow and actually rewired a room improperly, which required Lydia and her husband to move out while the problem was being corrected. Although the builder paid for the problem he had caused, Lydia had to live with her in-laws for over two months! There's no way of knowing whether the process would have been smoother if she'd had the builder of her choice, but in retrospect Lydia's husband probably wishes he'd acquiesced. Trusting your builder can pay off enormously in the amount of comfort you'll have during the process, and the final outcome will be celebrated with genuine joy instead of reluctant relief.

Beyond deciding who will do the work, you will have to face making many other decisions as well, some that will seem inconsequential at the time but are actually very important. For instance, when you are asked which kind of doorknob to use, you may think it's not a big deal, yet everyday living can be highly challenging if your three-year-old is always taking it apart or a poor choice constantly won't catch. Details are annoying and it's human nature to overlook them until the last minute. My friend Alice used a blanket spell to cover herself for this very reason. Alice has an excellent conceptual mind but lacks practical follow-through. She cast a spell (conceptualizing is great for spells) and asked that she be guided through all of the details ahead of her. Happily, she reports that all of her choices, including the last-minute kitchen counters she'd forgotten to choose, all work with her taste and concept—and she didn't break her budget.

On yet another level, changing your home can impact you deeply.

When you change your home, take a look at your life and how you, too, are undergoing "renovation."

For Lydia, the disruption of her home life that had her staying with her in-laws coincided with some changes she was making in her career, which she was trying to expand and shift into new directions. Lydia endured a lot of stress during the period of her renovation but came out of it with her home intact and new, firm ground in her working life.

Often, the work you do on your house is a reflection of the work you are doing somewhere else in your life. Don't be surprised if you have a strong reaction to seeing your furniture moved, walls stripped, and dust and dirt everywhere—it's hard to take this disruption to security. That's another reason why trust is so important.

MAINTENANCE

In more general spell work for hearth and home, you might just want to refresh the magic a bit, by giving the place a good dust-up, for example, or tackling spring housecleaning. Maintaining the atmosphere of your home and making it cozy and comfortable is always an ongoing effort. It's great once in a while to just take a moment and extend the energy of gratitude and support for your dwelling—like casting a spell for blessing the home.

Maintaining your home is a lot of work physically—cleaning, weatherproofing, painting, and so on. Maintaining your home's energetic character takes a more emotional and spiritual commitment. Here are a few tips for keeping the energy of your home from getting stilted, stuffy, or stifled.

- Keep organic things in as many rooms as possible—plants, stones, rocks, pieces of nature you may have collected.
- Move blankets, throw pillows, or art from the walls into different rooms—changing visual patterns can shift energy very swiftly.
- Keep plastics to a minimum, including plastic wrap for dry cleaning and plastic playthings.
- Open your windows and get air flowing.
- Play music—the airwaves carry great power when there's melody in them.

Spell for Psychic Housecleaning

This spell is preferably performed during a waning moon but can be cast as needed for cleansing during any moon phase.

Any evening after sunset,
light the end of a sagebrush stick.
Have a glass of water and a bowl
containing a shallow pool of water nearby.
Blow out the flame and blow on the embers
of the stick to increase the smoke.
In each room of your house,
blow smoke in each of the four directions.
Blow gently upon the burning stick
as you face each wall of the room.

Say aloud:
*I clear this space of all negativity
and of the energy of people or things
that have no purpose in our household.
I ask that this clearing be gentle
and that all of this energy be returned to its source.*

When you are done with your whole house,
return to the room you started in.
Take the stick and dip it into the shallow
bowl of water to douse the embers.
Take a sip of water from your glass.

Say aloud:
*This home is a gentle and supportive environment.
I offer gratitude to the universe that this is done.
So be it.
And so it is.*

Spell for Moving In

On a Thursday during a waxing moon*
and during the third hour after sunset,
light a white candle and a green candle.
Place a vase of local flowers next to the candles.
Place a picture, symbol, or mementos of the
people who will be living in this house
next to the flowers.
Have some bread and a glass of wine or water at hand.

Say aloud:

I call upon Vesta, goddess of hearth and home,
the elements of our planet, fire, earth, air, and water,
and the universal energy to witness this initiation.
I affirm that this home is blessed with love,
its inhabitants are supported and secure,
and this dwelling is blessed
by the energy of life and spirit.

Take a bite of bread and a sip of wine or water.

Say aloud:

We participate in the flow of prosperity
and respect the health and beauty
of the land that supports us.
We bless this house with our own energy and say,
So be it.
And so it is.

Let the candles burn as long as you want.
You can use them for other spells.

*This spell is preferably done on a waxing moon,
but if it must be performed during the waning moon,
follow the correct planetary hour.

Blessing and Maintaining Your Home

This spell can be performed during any moon cycle and can be
repeated as often as you like.

On a Sunday after sunset,
light a white candle.
Place your favorite flowers
in a vase with water.
Place pictures of your family
near the candle.

Say aloud:
*I ask the powers of the universe to
continue to bless this home and
keep all of its inhabitants in the flow of the universe.
I extend gratitude to the elements for supporting
our house and to Vesta for continuing to fuel our hearth.*

Close your eyes. From your heart center, send the energy of
love into every room of your house. Surround your entire
house with love in your mind's eye.

Say aloud:
*Blessings from my heart for this home.
So be it.
And so it is.*

Spell for Safety and Security

On a Monday during a waxing moon and
in the first hour after sunset,
light a pink candle and a white one.
Place a handful of basil
in a vessel made of organic materials.
Place pink or white roses in a vase with water.

Say aloud:
I ask the universe to join me
in manifesting safety and security for
my home and on my property.
I affirm that we are part of a greater energy,
and flow with its mystery and magnificence.
I ask that this place be protected and
secure from negativity and intrusion and
I participate in keeping its peace.

Walk around your home and grounds,
sprinkling basil in each room and outside
in each direction, north, west, south, and east.

Back inside, say:
So be it.
And so it is.

Blow out your candles.
When the roses are no longer fresh,
throw the petals around your property.

Spell for Changing Your Home: Trust

On a Monday during a waxing moon and
in the first hour after sunset,
light a yellow candle.
Put two vases of carnations side by side.
Place cinnamon in a vessel made of organic materials.

Say aloud:
*I call upon Vesta, the guardians,
and the great cosmic energy
to aid me in this project.
In expanding our home we expand
our heart center,
our life force.
I ask that the right person
aid us in this great task and
that all choices be guided
by the greater good.
We create together a home of
beauty, security, and endurance.*

Take some carnations out of one vase
and put them into the other.

Say aloud:
*I turn this over to the universe
with love and say,
So be it.
And so it is.*

Leave the cinnamon in the house while the work
is being done.

Enchantments for Every Room

General Spell for Holding Energy

Spell for Ease and Camaraderie (Dining Room)

Spell for Playfulness (Family Room)

Spell for Sacred Space (Bedroom)

Spell for Nurturing and Love (Kids' Rooms)

Spell for Welcoming (New-Baby Room)

Spell for Health and Joy for Grandparents

Spell for Commitment and Honesty
with Domestic Help

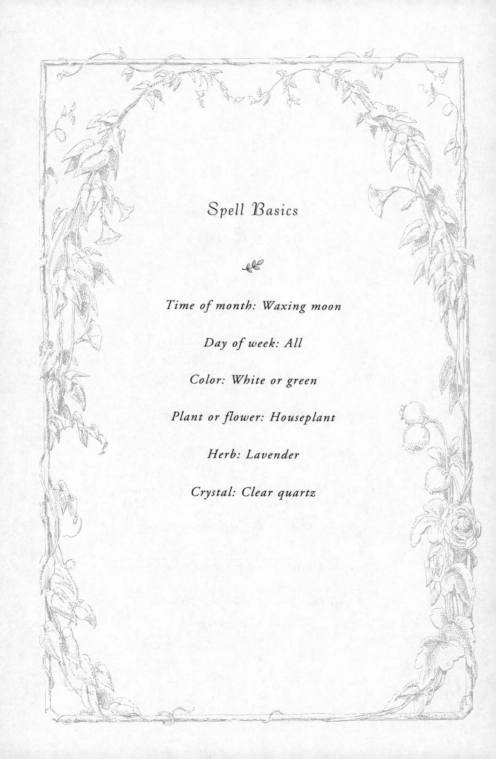

Spell Basics

Time of month: Waxing moon

Day of week: All

Color: White or green

Plant or flower: Houseplant

Herb: Lavender

Crystal: Clear quartz

$\mathcal{E}$very room in your house already holds its own personality and atmosphere. Some of this aura has to do with you and your emotional life, while some of it relates to visitors and other beings in the room. Much of a room's energy comes from the things within it—furniture, fabric, objects. You may find one room magnetic yet another room repulsive, but when you know about how to enchant a room, you can make any space into a place you'll want to be.

Before we get started conjuring, take a toll of the psychic energy your house holds already. Survey the room you use most often. Note how many (if any) of the following elements you have.

The A List

_____ 1. Photos of family members or pets

_____ 2. Natural fibers in carpets

_____ 3. Natural fibers for bedding, blankets, and curtains

_____ 4. Lamps

_____ 5. Plants

_____ 6. Personal mementos

_____ 7. A mirror

_____ 8. Artwork

_____ 9. Books

_____10. Metal

_____11. Windows that open

_____12. Fragments of nature, including stones, shells, and pieces of wood (but not including dried flower arrangements unless you made them yourself from your own flowers)

_____13. Animals (your pets)

_____ Total

The B List

_____ 1. TV

_____ 2. Computer

_____ 3. Furniture made of plastic, Formica, vinyl, or other "man-made" materials

_____ 4. Silk flowers or artificial plants

_____ 5. Nylon carpets or rugs

_____ 6. Veneer or pressed wood

_____ 7. Artificial beams or molding

_____ 8. Plastic flowerpots

_____ 9. Plastic or man-made figurines

_____10. Artwork you don't like or care about

_____11. Objects or collectibles made from man-made materials

_____12. Fluorescent lights

_____13. No windows

_____   Total

If your B List outweighs your A List, you're living in less than ideal energy.

THE POWER OF THE A LIST: ORGANIC OR SYMBOLIC

A List items are organic or symbolic of supportive, nurturing energy; they interact with your unconscious to signal life and vitality. You don't have to clutter rooms with these objects and materials, but you should use them to some extent to "spruce up" your atmosphere. These items will help you feel psychically fit and energetic, and they can ground positive energy to keep it there for when you need it.

A photo of your family (one you like and feel positive about) keeps their energy alive and engenders a spirit of togetherness, even when you're apart.

Natural fibers, like cotton, wool, or silk, are organic; these fabrics come from nature and (metaphysically speaking) carry vibrations of life. Cotton breathes and keeps energy moving. Wool can be nurturing and warm—or a bit rough and rustic. Silk brings luxury, allure, and mystery—it cloaks energy to contain it. Man-made fibers and materials don't have these properties. They may keep you warm, protect your floors, or add texture to your environment, but they come from a conglomeration of oil and chemicals and don't carry with them properties of energy enhancement.

Lamps, though they aren't alive and are not necessarily organic, are symbols of illumination and are very powerful triggers to our unconscious selves. Lamps have long been a symbol of wisdom and enlightenment.

Plants, of course, are great providers of life vibration.

Personal mementos, too, can be supportive, especially if they hold extraordinary meaning: your child's handprint in clay, your grandfather's antique barometer—these things help you underscore the love, support, and tradition of your home and family.

A mirror reflects energy. And while usually mirrors help the energy of a room, too many mirrors or those that reflect glare can "burn you out" with too much light.

Artwork provides symbols, color, and flavor to your home. As long as you aren't plastering your walls with meaningless paintings, drawings, or prints, you're getting something back from your art.

Books are a symbol of wisdom (something we can all use around the house) and provide a cozy atmosphere, as in an old library.

Eastern philosophies treat metals as a separate element. Ores and metals found in the earth are very energetically powerful, so they carry some nice vibrations and can add a unique power to a room (bars on jail cells excepted). My favorites are gold, silver, and copper, but mixes and alloys, such as bronze, tin, or pewter, all contribute stability, resilience, and strength to a room's atmosphere.

🌿 Windows are found in many rooms in your home, but they're useless if they don't open. Windows work both to "see" out of and to change the atmosphere of the room, but they have to permit air to flow in order to do that.

🌿 The two most powerful things you can have in your home are the bits of nature you happen to find as keepsakes and the animals you may have chosen to care for. Any connections you make with your heart to things in nature, whether alive like animals or "dead" like stones, anchor strong and positive heart energy in your home. They are personal, powerful, supportive, and there for a reason, even if you don't know what that reason is.

THE B LIST: A DRAIN ON YOUR RESOURCES

If the B List is more prevalent in your favorite room, your energy is not being refreshed or regenerated. While you are relaxing, allowing your psyche to just "be," you're putting out your psychic energy without thinking about it. This openness and rest should be restorative, but when you don't have enough energetic or psychic circulation, you won't necessarily get the benefits. Man-made things generally don't have any vibration, so they don't interact with your energy. You'll be allowing your precious energy to flow out and getting nothing in return. Additionally, your home may not be as "safe" as you might like.

🌿 TV and computer equipment can drain your rooms of energy.

They are almost always encased in plastic, inorganic material, and they also provide electronic "buzz," which can mess with a supportive, nurturing atmosphere and even your aura. If you don't understand what I mean, go to an appliance store. Even if there are comfortable chairs in which to sit, a room full of computers or televisions is neither cozy nor comfortable—in fact, you may find it disconcerting. On the other hand, try going to a furniture store (one with real wood or leather) and you might find an easier atmosphere, and one in which you could hang around longer.

   ✤ I don't include stereo equipment as a deterrence to your home's atmosphere because the energy of music far outweighs the machine's opposition.

   ✤ You may think it's peculiar to shun silk flowers after I've gone on about organic materials, but unfortunately, silk flowers are often dusty and ignored and are poor substitutes for the real thing. Even dried flower bouquets lose their powers when they become obscured or forgotten.

   ✤ Nylon rugs and carpets, particle wood veneer, artificial beams, and molding are all cost-effective decorative choices, but they don't add to the power of your atmosphere. Go ahead and use them, but you'll find it more pleasant to employ such materials sparingly—the same goes for man-made or plastic figurines.

   ✤ I know plastic flowerpots are convenient and nice (and I've even used them myself from time to time), but if you have too many plastics, you might not feel that lovely energy your plants are giving you. Try plaster, terra cotta, or porcelain—heavier but much more grounded in life vibrations.

   ✤ Artwork can add dramatically to the energy of a room, or it can add nothing whatsoever. If you don't like your artwork or if you have it "just because it matches the couch," it isn't worth having. You don't get any benefit for your atmosphere. Be sure to hang a picture you really like, even if it doesn't match your decor.

Most of us have homes with a mixture of A and B elements. If you do find yourself lacking in the A category, your home may be more of a drain on your energy than a sanctuary where you can rest, refresh, and revitalize. The "dialogue" your body and your unconscious have with A List elements is very life-affirming—you are very much a part of nature, and living among its elements is beneficial. Packing yourself up in a home full of man-made materials, on the other hand, can deaden your connection to nature, which in turn diminishes your life force, psychic energy, and vitality.

Dead Rooms

I recently visited a house where there was a lot of wood furniture, windows, light, and natural fabrics—quite heavily an A List home. The room most often used was a sun porch, made of cedar, decorated with lots of teak furniture with cotton cushions. But this room was dead as a doornail. Why?

Dead rooms can feel inert in spite of being filled and pulsing with organic energy. This results from a lack of connection to the people.

You can find a dead room anywhere—like the living room where nobody goes because "it's only for company," or the guest room where even rambunctious kids won't play because it's so still and "empty."

Dead rooms happen not only when the materials found in them are inorganic, but when either nobody uses them or their inhabitants are depressed, repressed, or numb. Dead rooms are a strong and silent comment on your household—and are not welcoming. A dead room is useful if you don't want guests to overstay their welcome, but in most cases, it's best to enliven the room with some energy.

Every room in your house can produce its own energy and personality. Painting the walls and arranging furniture is a beginning, but there's more you can do. You can implant your heart energy in a room or even in just a tiny space—and ground it there.

As I've already mentioned, in recent experience I was challenged to create a separate and very special space: a baby's room. When our daughter Elisabeth arrived, there was really no "room" for her, but of course we wanted to dedicate a space to her. We did have the benefit of a great walk-in closet, which, upon consideration and a lot of measuring, we chose to make into a "baby alcove." It didn't escape our notice that we were going to put our newborn into a closet, so we set about its transformation with care. First we took the two doors off the closet to make a real alcove—not a closet. Then we prepared her little space lovingly, with sunny yellow paint, lots of soft animals on high shelves, a softly lit wall lamp, and a beautiful handmade mobile for her to gaze upon in her newborn stupor. There was no room for the usual baby things—a changing table or a rocking chair—but we did squeeze in a small chest of drawers.

Her "room," referred to as the Baby Alcove, was done. It looked cozy and sweet—but it needed something else. I kept feeling that there was something missing. Many of you already know that welcoming a newborn is a delicate process; newborns are easily startled at their abrupt arrival in this light, noisy, and cold world. They are also so sensitive that they can really feel vibrations and energy in a room. And so, with the help of my colleagues, after Elisabeth came home, we enchanted her Baby Alcove to help her adjust to this world.

As with all spells, there's no way of telling how effective this was, but I think it helped her and I know it helped me. By placing a symbol of each element around her crib—an orange citrine for fire, a jade egg for earth, a clear crystal for air, and a starfish skeleton for water—I asked the universe to help anchor her here. As I placed these elements, I cast a spell for creating a space in which Elisabeth could adapt to the world gently and smoothly.

The spell I performed for the Baby Alcove is an example of how to ground an environment with a certain kind of energy. With your heart, you send the love you feel or the intention you have into the room and anchor it there with elements, candles, and/or symbols of what you want. These types of spells are active rituals whereby your actions and words work up magic to create the basic energy of a room.

One of the tricks for ensuring the success of these spells is the anchoring process. You'll use an object in each spell that you should leave in the room after you're done. This object will hold the energy of your magic and keep it anchored there for as long as you need it. You'll learn to use anchoring in many ways once you get skillful with it, and you'll find it's very handy for keeping things consistent in a chaotic environment.

ENCHANTMENTS BY ROOM

The spells in this chapter are designed to give you a blueprint to work with—I certainly haven't covered all that you might want to do in the rooms of your home. I encourage you to be creative with your spells. Here are the basics you'll need.

1. First, you'll need to know the purpose of the room (its primary use).

2. Then you'll need to determine the kind of emotional quality you'd like your room to hold.
3. Finally, you'll need objects that represent this emotional quality.

From here, you just identify the day of the week that helps your purpose (see page 33) and the color that best suits your emotional quality. You'll have the best results if you use a plant in your spell and leave that in the room as well as your anchor object.

Your first spell may not be quite as dramatic as one called for when preparing a newborn's room. You can perform a spell for almost any room and for any purpose. I've included spells here that are the most commonly used. For instance, you might want to make a room you use often open to camaraderie—or, conversely, you can cast a spell to make a room sacred and respected for its privacy. Keep in mind that these spells infuse a room with its basic energy and, if it's a room that's used regularly, it will take on a subtle dynamic that will support and enhance its personality.

SPECIAL SPELLS FOR THE HOUSEHOLD

Also included in this chapter are two unusual spells that focus on people who may be part of your household periodically but not permanently. Grandparents are often part of the household on occasion, or in some cases they may even live there, but their energy may require a somewhat different atmosphere than yours. Also, domestic help, whether live-in or live-out, definitely contributes to your household's energy, and anyone who has ever had a nasty housekeeper or sullen maid will underscore how important their serenity is to yours.

Grandparents bring a great deal of atmosphere and warmth to your home (even if you don't feel it directly) by the nature of their attachment to you and to the past. You might find that grandparents can be draining or somehow a strain on you—for many reasons. Aside from the obvious maladies of age like slower movement or memory loss, grandparents exercise their right to an opinion (even unsolicited) and respect. It's not always easy to find the time and the good graces to give them what they need, and spells can be very helpful in enhancing their experience in your household. Whether they're staying with you or living with you, you can make them feel at home and well supported without straining your own resources. The more often you see them, the more need you'll have for a spell of this nature, in order to create a blanket of nurturing, embracing, healthy energy for them without having to constantly re-create it. When grandparents visit only occasionally, you're more likely to treat it as a special occasion, and, hence, a spell can ensure a special, memorable experience.

Domestic help is a very different issue. When you pay someone to be a part of your household, whether it's as a cleaner, caretaker, driver, nanny, or gardener, his or her energy is very important to your well-being. Imagine a hostile gardener keeping your grounds for you, infusing his anger or discontent into your land. Or consider your child's nanny—if he or she isn't at ease in your household, how can your child feel secure? It's all too common to find people treating domestic help without consideration or compassion, and this is just bad karma. You can cast one simple spell for commitment and honesty for your domestic staff, and the universe should help your relationship with them to remain healthy or, in the worst-case scenario, help you remove them from your home.

These spells for grandparents and domestic help are different from the others in this book, since they are aimed at people, not rooms, events, or occasions. In this case your heart energy and focus need to be impeccable, and your own integrity counts heavily. Your participation in these spells will have strong effects on your behavior and your household's atmosphere, so do them wisely. You must be genuine in your intention, open to your foibles or laziness, and allow these members of your household to feel as if they belong. You're likely to find that you have mixed feelings as you perform these spells, but don't worry—you won't be asking them to stay for eternity. All you're doing is creating the psychic space for them to be in your home now for the good of all concerned.

General Spell for Holding Energy*

On any night during a waxing moon,
light a green candle.
Next to the candle,
place a plant and an object that will stay
in the room you are working on.
Have a pitcher of water at hand.

Say aloud:
*I ask Vesta and the Universe to join
me in placing and holding this _____ energy
in this room.
I affirm the power of the elements,
fire, earth, air, and water,
to grow and hold this _____ energy in place.
I place water in this plant as a symbol of my
heartfelt intention* [water the plant],
*and I lay my hand on this object as a gesture
of grounding this life energy here in this room*
[lay your hand on the object].
*I ask that this be done for the greater good.
So be it.
And so it is.*

Blow out the candle.
Leave the plant and the object in that room.

You can keep the candle in this room and light it to
"reenergize" the spell, or you can use it later for another room.

*When reciting the spell, say the type of energy you want to
hold in place, like "joyful energy" or "healing energy" or
"passionate energy."

Spell for Ease and Camaraderie
(Dining Room)

On a Wednesday night during the second hour after sunset,
light a pink candle in the room you are enchanting.
Place some dry lavender and
a wineglass with water in it next to the candle.

Say aloud:
*On this evening of Mercury's power, I ask Venus
to bless this room with ease and camaraderie.
I ask that all who come here experience light and support
to enjoy the company of others, be comfortable,
and share their energy with consciousness.
I contribute my own energy to this room with the
intention that this be so.*

Drink a sip from the wineglass. Leave the lavender in the
room or sprinkle it in the four corners of the room.

Say aloud:
*So be it.
And so it is.*

Blow out the candle. Keep it in that room and relight
it once every moon cycle or as often as you feel you
need to. (You don't have to light it every time you
use the room.)

Spell for Playfulness (Family Room)

On a Wednesday during a waxing moon
and in the second hour after sunset,
light a yellow candle.
Place daisies, dandelions, or another kind of
yellow flower in a vase with water.

Say aloud:
I ask the Universe on this eve of Mercury in the hour of Venus
to bring the energy of playful exchanges and merriment
into this room. I affirm that there is much joy
and lightness in our lives and that we take time
to know and take pleasure in these gifts.
I bless this room and infuse it with fun.
I ask that this be done for the greater good
and that all who enter may take with them some light.
So be it.
And so it is.

Blow out the candle.

Spell for Sacred Space (Bedroom)

On a Sunday after sunset or on an evening of a new moon,
light a white candle.
Place a picture of the person or persons who use this room
and a clear quartz crystal next to the candle.
Have some flowers you like in a vase with water.
Keep a small bowl of sea salt at hand.

Say aloud:
*I call upon the universe
and great energies of the elements to
create this sacred space. I affirm that
this space holds supportive, loving energy and that
it serves as a haven for
[say the names of the people whose room it is].
This candle purifies this room and
this crystal resonates with their energy.*

Take the sea salt and sprinkle a little bit in a line
along the doorway and in front of any windows.

Say aloud:
*I purify this space and keep it safe
and sacred.
So be it.
And so it is.*

Blow out the candle. Keep all the spell elements in that room.
Keep the flower petals even after they've dried out; they can
hold the energy for some time.

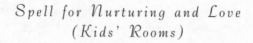

Spell for Nurturing and Love
(Kids' Rooms)

On a Monday during a waxing moon
and in the first hour after sunset,
light a pink candle.
Place lavender in a bowl made of organic materials
and an object of yours* that you can leave in the room
next to the candle. Have a glass of water at hand.

Say aloud:
On this loving, mystical Monday
and guided by the hour of Venus,
I ask that universal powers join me
in imbuing this room with love and support.
May the souls who rest here be protected and blessed,
and may they know they are loved.
With this lavender I create the space for open hearts.
With this object I ground my love and intention.
I drink this water as a symbol of participating in this love.

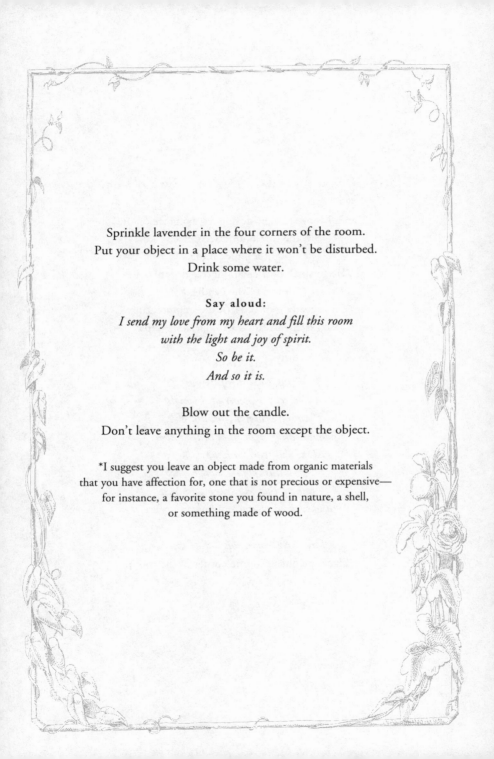

Sprinkle lavender in the four corners of the room.
Put your object in a place where it won't be disturbed.
Drink some water.

Say aloud:
I send my love from my heart and fill this room
with the light and joy of spirit.
So be it.
And so it is.

Blow out the candle.
Don't leave anything in the room except the object.

*I suggest you leave an object made from organic materials
that you have affection for, one that is not precious or expensive—
for instance, a favorite stone you found in nature, a shell,
or something made of wood.

Spell for Welcoming (New-Baby Room)

On a Monday night during a waxing moon and
in the first hour after sunset,*
light a pink candle.
Place a small houseplant and a glass of water
next to the candle.
Have ready four objects, one representing
each element: fire, earth, air, and water.

Say aloud:
Venus, bless this precious site
and let the power of the night
conjure comfort, health, love,
and healing light from heaven above.
Make this world a happy place and
keep this room a sacred space
to help this baby sleep with ease
and wake and grow and play in peace.

Fire, I call upon you to fuel this life.
Place fire object in one corner of the room.

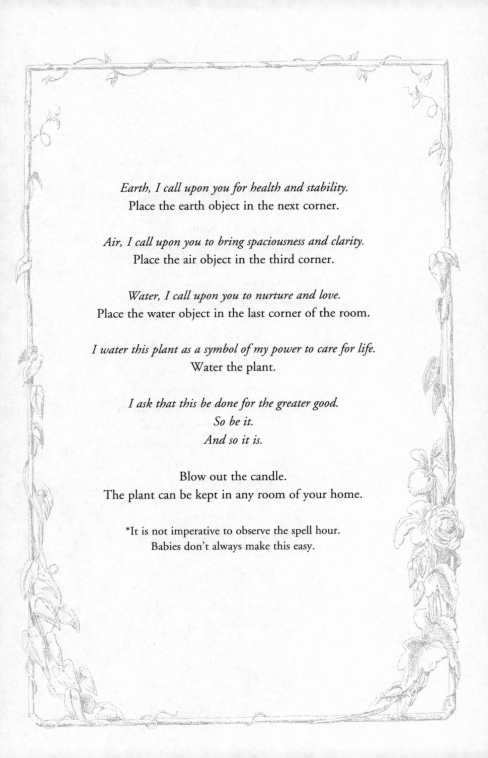

Earth, I call upon you for health and stability.
Place the earth object in the next corner.

Air, I call upon you to bring spaciousness and clarity.
Place the air object in the third corner.

Water, I call upon you to nurture and love.
Place the water object in the last corner of the room.

I water this plant as a symbol of my power to care for life.
Water the plant.

I ask that this be done for the greater good.
So be it.
And so it is.

Blow out the candle.
The plant can be kept in any room of your home.

*It is not imperative to observe the spell hour.
Babies don't always make this easy.

Spell for Health and Joy for Grandparents

On a Sunday during a waxing moon and in the
first hour after sunset,
light a white candle.
Place some flowers in a vase with water,
set out a photo of the grandparents,
and put caraway seeds or nutmeg in a bowl
made of organic materials.

Say aloud:
*Under the healing vibration of this
blessed Sunday and the power of Jupiter's hour,
I call upon the universe to join with me in
conjuring health and joy for these grandparents.
I ask that our home support their needs,
that they feel empowered, alive, and independent,
and that the love we feel for each other is steady
and ever present.
I ask that this be done for the greater good of
all those involved and with the blessing of
Vesta, goddess of hearth and home.
So be it.
And so it is.*

Leave the caraway or nutmeg in the house
until the full moon.

Spell for Commitment and Honesty
with Domestic Help

On a Saturday during a waxing moon and in the
first hour after sunset,
light a white candle and a blue candle.
Place some bay leaf, clove, and nutmeg
in a vessel made of an organic material.
Place some white flowers in a vase with water.

Say aloud:
*I bring in the constructive energy of Saturn
with the facility of communications of Mercury
in creating the energy of commitment and honesty
for our domestic help.
I ask that this household be protected and safe
from negativity and gossip and
that those who come to help are loyal.
I affirm that I respect their rights as people
and will create an atmosphere where work can be
done with ease, grace, and openness.
I ask that Vesta bestow her blessings and say,
So be it.
And so it is.*

Blow out the candle.
Throw the herbs out on the full moon.

General Atmosphere Enhancers

Spell for Coziness

Spell for Liveliness

Spell for Healing

Spell for Easing Tension

A Spell to Study

Mood Shifting for Fire Signs

Mood Shifting for Earth Signs

Mood Shifting for Air Signs

Mood Shifting for Water Signs

Spell Basics

Author's Note:
There are no spell basics in this chapter
because each spell and mood shifter
require very specific directions.

*A*s you've learned, spells are great ways to set up the basic pulse of your house, as well as of each individual room, and to make an environment more conducive to certain activities. Yet spells do require a certain amount of preparation, timing, and focus that can prevent you from making spontaneous changes or adjustments to your atmospheres. For those times when what you have in mind is a quick change, there are things you can do that don't require a full-blown spell, but still shift energy and create ambiance.

The fastest and easiest way to shift the atmosphere of a room is to alter one of the elements in it: fire, earth, air, or water. Consider how these elements might make a room feel different:

- Candlelight
- Plush, colorful blanket throws
- Incense
- Music

Each of the above contributes a new layer of energy to a room, and each shifts a different elemental power. Remember, each element plays with the senses in a different way.

FIRE

Fire brings out a number of atmospheric energies, among them passion, illumination, and warmth. A roaring fire in the hearth produces an altogether different kind of energy than glowing embers, and candlelight casts a totally different mood than electric light. Fire also represents purification, as when white candles are used for rituals, or bonfires (or hearth fires) are used to burn old things. When you use fire, pay attention to its intensity and purpose. If you simply want a gentle warmth or an accent on passion, use it sparingly. If, on the other hand, you're going for a greater energy or more impactful atmosphere, you can push the fire element further by using more of it.

EARTH

Earth is the steadiness and coziness of being embraced, like having a soft warm blanket wrapped around you. Earth reminds us that we are supported and that the literal ground beneath our feet and the fields that grow our crops help us sustain life. Earth is less likely to shift (unless it's sand or it's being pushed around by other elements), so earth can naturally make you feel more secure. It takes a great deal of effort to go too far with the earth element, but people *can* do too much: too much food, too many decorations or objects, too much stuff. Too much earth can be suffocating just as too little can be uncomfortable. All physical elements in your home are earth symbols, even when they are in place because of their other elemental qualities, like crystals, which are objects for air. While being too spare with the earth element can make your home feel inhospitable, be aware that too much of it can be an avalanche and make your household feel encumbered.

AIR

The elemental quality of air is transparent (usually), but it carries significant energy to your atmosphere. For instance, there's nothing worse than a stinky household odor, nor is there anything more relaxing than a delicious smell coming from the kitchen. Olfactory perception conjures real mood reaction and memory, which is why it is so important to your atmosphere. Temperature is also very important, particularly when a room is hot and stuffy, which makes people lose energy, or when a room is cold, which usually is unwelcoming. Air can be crystal clear, foggy, heavy, or thin. Pay attention to the air of your household to keep it healthy and circulating.

WATER

Water is emotional. How can water, something you don't have present in every room, affect atmosphere? As the element of emotion, water carries mood. Look around for what contributes to mood in your home, and that's where your water element is. Sometimes the water element is your color scheme—soft and muted, vibrant and loud, varying, monochromatic, or dark. Color contributes to your emotional atmosphere by the tone it sets. Music is another powerful water element. Music and sound can raise or lower the vibration of your home. Many of us already use music to shift moods, but now that you're aware of its importance as a water element, you can use it more often and more consciously.

Shifting your atmosphere is not hard, but you do need to be skillful in how you combine all the elements at hand. Too many elements or too much of one can result in overkill.

Years ago, I visited San Francisco and stayed in an old bed-and-breakfast in the heart of the city. The place was run by two middle-aged men who obviously took great care of their Victorian house and who relished sharing their home with their paying guests. The house was in great condition. Its ice-cream colors, delicate details, and varnished wood interiors were inviting from what I could see from the street, but once I stepped into that house, I couldn't wait to get out. I stayed only one night, and at the time I couldn't understand my "allergy" to the place.

The entry hall was fine—spacious, sparsely furnished, lit by one standing lamp at the far end. The parlor, where the guests came to relax and speak to their hosts, was Victorian in all its grandeur—potted palms, dark silk walls, deep sofas, wing chairs, and a lot of disparate stuff, including old dolls, some sort of antique wooden toy (I had no idea what it was), a full set of vintage fire tools in front of a nonworking fireplace, cushions, gas lamps, candles, screens, and knickknacks galore. A heavy scent of cloves filled the air, and out of some invisible tape player came Victorian dance hall music. That room made me feel that I was in constant danger of knocking down something expensive and irreplaceable, and the music and scent put me on edge.

Escaping to my bedroom would be a relief, I thought—until I saw my room. Sadly, each bedroom suffered at the hands of the overeager decorator-hosts. I got the "old doll room," or so I called it. It was filled with creepy porcelain-faced dolls in dusty old dresses, along with lots of potpourri (spicy-scented), old cushions, lamps, china bits and pieces, and not a single empty space to rest my book next to the bed. The antique quilts were lovely, and granted, there were some nice things in the room. But the next morning, after a hearty English breakfast (admittedly a high point), I checked out.

I've since realized that the discomfort I felt had a great deal to do with the overloaded elemental combination of earth and water—which left very little room for air or fire. Generally, overkill comes from too much of one or more elements. My hosts went overboard with their enthusiasm for the Victorian period and their appetite for collecting period things, which led to too much earth (being "buried alive") and water ("drowning" in mood). Since there was very little air, I felt suffocated, and the lack of the fire element sapped my energy. This was an unpleasant elemental combination, to say the least.

You've seen overkill atmospheres before, like weddings where every single element, from the place cards to the centerpieces—even the dessert!—are coordinated with lovey-dovey themes, or at Christmas, the holiday that begs for overkill, when an entire house can be "over-atmosphered" and there's so much decoration, food, drink, and music that you feel full before you're even in the door.

Atmospheres can be very delicate things, and achieving the correct balance in them is an art. If you remember the fundamental reason for an atmosphere, you are less likely to create overkill:

> *Atmospheres provide support and encouragement to create—not dictate—a good time for your family and guests.*

Atmospheres are not supposed to spoon-feed jolliness or communicate a hard-hitting message. The most effective atmospheres are the least detectable. Guests can be put on guard if they feel they are "expected" to react in a certain way.

INADVERTENT ATMOSPHERE KILLERS

While overloading elements and creating an uncomfortable atmosphere may not happen so frequently, there are many seemingly minor household things that can kill an atmosphere quite effectively.

Televisions
Walk into any home at any time and find the TV on: atmosphere killer. That house could be pulsing with positive vibes, psychically supportive and attuned, but you wouldn't notice because that television virtually numbs your senses to those subtle vibrations. I'm not anti-television at all, but if you're hoping to create a specific atmosphere—unless, of course, your "theme" revolves around a TV show, like the broadcast of the Super Bowl or the Miss America pageant—don't leave the TV on when no one is watching.

Phones
Telephones are an important part of our lives, no doubt, but they can be unwelcome intruders when you are trying to maintain an atmosphere. Even when you need to be available in case of an emergency, you don't need to have every telephone in the house on high-pitch ring. Rather than have the phone startle your guests or yourself into a state of "alert," try keeping it in another room within hearing distance, or better still, turn it off. People who need to be reached usually carry cellular phones or beepers—which are yet more atmosphere wreckers but not within your control.

Computers
Computers are also guilty of atmosphere murder. Just seeing a computer with a blank screen or a screen saver reminds you that there's

something else to do. A computer can be very distracting—and even more so if someone starts playing a video game.

Air Freshener

Since I live in New York City and take cabs quite often, I am particularly sensitive to the artificial fragrances that are supposed to cover up foul odors. I really don't know what's worse, nasty organic smells or artificial cover-ups. Room fresheners are often just too pronounced to be subtle and too formulated to be natural. If you use them, your atmosphere will be heavy with scent and light on connection.

Random Appliances

This may seem odd to you, but I've walked into households where an iron was sitting on the dining-room table or a vacuum cleaner's been left out in the family room. Again: atmosphere killers. Even silly little things like a Dustbuster or battery recharger ruin atmosphere. The utilitarian messages these appliances send do not contribute to any kind of positive energy. (Of course, when you're actually doing it, sometimes things like ironing or vacuuming can make you feel well taken care of or cozy—but don't *over*do it.)

YOUR MOOD

Along with the inadvertent atmosphere killers cited above is a far more important and serious atmospheric influence: you. If you're the host or head of the household (and I mean head of running the household), your mood permeates every room, every nook, every corner of your home. If your mood is rotten, you can bet the household knows it.

You can't be expected to be full of merry sunshine every day, or even just to stay balanced. After all, despite the magical spell-casting you've been doing, you're still human. Your moods are going to change, and you are certainly entitled to them. However, it can be quite distressing to find yourself in a bad mood when you really want things to go well; your atmosphere will fade as your mood darkens. If you've been putting a lot of energy into your atmosphere (like cleaning and decorating and adjusting tiny details), you might find yourself spent of energy, and this depletion can negatively affect your atmosphere if you're not careful.

One of my clients always shakes off what she calls her "preparation energy" by taking a quick walk around the block before her guests come. Much to her husband's annoyance, she sometimes returns right when their guests are arriving. She claims her husband's fleeting irritation is worth the "fresh spirit" she feels when she returns to her own home like a party guest.

Astrological Mood Antidotes

Once you find yourself in a nasty mood, it's hard to pull out of it. Negativity breeds inertia, which makes it all that much harder to "snap out of it" or take some action to feel better. You can try to smudge yourself in case you happen to have picked up someone else's toxicity, and you can try to center yourself to keep your mood from spilling over onto others. But if nothing works, I recommend doing a mood-enhancing activity using your astrological sign as your guide.

Your astrological sign corresponds to one of the elements. By using your element, you can regain some positive vibes, if not some downright zeal for the moment at hand. Chances are you don't have the time or inclination to do a really specific spell when in a bad mood, but astrological mood antidotes aren't really spells. Still, they do work on amplifying your personal magic and magnetism enough to replenish the energy of your natural element and keep you from being your own worst enemy.

While you'll find these mood shifters at the end of this chapter, you can also think about making up your own. The basic idea behind these mood adjusters is to "take in" your primary elemental energy. Find your element by locating your astrological sign in the chart below.

Sign	Element
Aries	Fire
Taurus	Earth
Gemini	Air
Cancer	Water
Leo	Fire
Virgo	Earth
Libra	Air
Scorpio	Water
Sagittarius	Fire
Capricorn	Earth
Aquarius	Air
Pisces	Water

When you're in need of a lift, get in touch with your element. For instance, if you're a Cancer, a water sign, try washing your face with water, drinking a glass of water, or, if possible, looking out at a body of water or a fish tank. If you're a Leo, a fire sign, stick your face into the sun (briefly) and breathe in the light, or gaze into a match flame and open up to its heat. An air sign like Libra would benefit from a brief walk outside for a change of air, and an earth sign like Capricorn would find holding a precious object energizing.

These simple moments to enhance your mood can infuse you with enough energy to get you out of the darkness and into the light. Others, too, will benefit by your mood shift, so give it a try.

ELEMENTS AND THEIR SYMBOLS

To help you create atmospheres and shift moods, learn to identify things that bring different elemental energy to your home—below is a list of some of them. You can use these in your household when you want to push the energy of that element forward. Just familiarizing yourself with the elements will make you more skillful at creating atmospheres in general.

Fire
Candles
Hearth fires
Wood-burning stoves
Lamps
The colors red, orange, and yellow
Citrine
Carnelian
Garnet
Bay leaf
Cinnamon

Earth
Any organic objects, furniture, or fabrics except silk
Plants
The colors green and brown
Jade

Jasper
Agate
Marble
Wood
Tulips

Air
All scents and fragrances
Air conditioning, fans, or heating
The colors blue and purple
Incense
Smoke
Almonds, Brazil nuts, and pecans
Lavender
Mint
Lapis lazuli
Clear quartz crystal

Water
Music or sounds
Silk fabric
The color white or metallic colors, as well as some sea greens
Aquariums or fishbowls
Moonstone
Opals
Amethyst
Apples, grapes, peaches, pears, and lemons
Daisies
Eucalyptus

Spell for Coziness

On a Monday during a waning moon
and in the first hour after sunset,
light a yellow candle.
Place a bunch of grapes next to
a pitcher of water.
Place a cinnamon stick next to the grapes.

Say aloud:
*I honor Vesta with the flame of joy
and gather in the blessings of ancient
hearth and home to create
an atmosphere of love, support, and nurturing.
May all beings who come here feel
the warmth, care, and coziness of Vesta's flame
and honor her, too, with their heart and faith.
May this be done for healing and health,
for the greater good of all.
So be it.
And so it is.*

Eat some grapes. Drink some water and use it to
water plants. Leave the cinnamon stick in the room where it
won't be disturbed. Relight the candle whenever you want to
infuse the room with more cozy energy.

Spell for Liveliness

On a Tuesday during a waxing moon and in the
second hour after sunset,
light a red candle.
Place some orange flowers in a vase with water.
Put some tea in a vessel made from organic substances and
place it next to the candle.

Say aloud:

*May Mars's fiery energy join with me in this expansive
time to conjure the energy of vitality and liveliness.
I ask that the beings in this room enjoy strength, energy,
and wellness guided by Vesta's firm hand and blessing.
May life be fully expressed and enjoyed within these walls.
For the greater good, I say,
So be it.
And so it is.*

Leave the candle burning until you are done in the room.
Throw out the tea on the full moon. Use the candle again
when you want to renew the atmosphere of the room.

Spell for Healing

On a Sunday during a waxing moon*
and in the first hour after sunset,
light a white candle and a purple candle.
Have a houseplant and some water at hand.
If desired, place photos or objects of people or things
you wish to receive healing next to the candle.
Place some walnuts next to the plant.

Say aloud:
On this day of healing and blessing and
in the open hour of Jupiter,
I ask that all beings, guides, guardians,
and angels join with me to endow
healing into this room.
I ask that those in need of health find
balance within their bodies, and those
whose hearts are wounded find solace.
May the energy of healing and serenity
ease all who rest here.
I ask that this is done for the greater good.
So be it.
And so it is.

Leave the candle burning as long as you use the room.
Water the plant and any others in the room.
Leave the walnuts in a place where they won't be disturbed.
Repeat during the next waxing moon.

*This can be done during a waning moon if necessary.

Spell for Easing Tension

On a Friday during a waxing moon
and in the second hour after sunset,
light a pink candle and a blue candle.
Place some lavender in a vessel made of organic materials.
If possible, place some fresh basil next to the candles.
Put some pink flowers in a vase with water.

Say aloud:
May the loving energy of Venus
and the healing power of the Sun
ease and soothe the energy of the beings in this space.
With blue, spacious calm and gentle pink light,
align the hearts and souls in sync with the energy
of life and support.

Place the lavender in the four corners of the room.
Inhale the fragrance of fresh basil.

Say aloud:
I ask that all beings join me in opening
space and time for soothing and easy breath.
For the greater good, I say,
So be it.
And so it is.

Light the candles whenever you want to strengthen the spell.

A Spell to Study

On a Saturday during any moon phase
and in the first hour after sunset,
light a blue candle.
Place some rosemary in a vessel made of organic materials.
Have a houseplant with a glass of water at hand.

Say aloud:
*May Saturn's structure and hard work permeate
the atmosphere of this room to give all who come here
the ability to concentrate and attend to work.
Blue energy of crystal-clear concentration opens the mind,
and Vesta's flame protects and sustains life.*

Place water in the houseplant and take some rosemary in
your hand and smell its fragrance.

Say aloud:
*As the plant thrives with water, so do minds
fill with knowledge.
Sharp minds and wits are supported within these
walls, for the greater good.
So be it.
And so it is.*

Leave the rosemary in the room. Light the candle
each time you want to concentrate.

Mood Shifting for Fire Signs

To increase your energy or uplift mood:

Sit in direct sunlight for at least two minutes.

Light a match and "breathe" in its flame.

Gaze at a fire (not embers).

Concentrate on feeling warmth in your solar plexus.

Eat something with hot spices.

To soften your energy or release your stress:

Visualize exhaling flame out of your solar plexus into
    a trash basket.

Drink a glass of water.

Sit still for at least five minutes.

Close your eyes or go into a dark room for a short time.

Mood Shifting for Earth Signs

To lift a bad mood or when feeling stuck:
Clap your hands hard together five times, then press them directly
    against the ground or floor for one minute.
Hold a clear crystal in your hands for at least two minutes.
Leave the room for more than five minutes.
Take a walk outside and touch some leaves or grass.

To help focus or concentrate your energy:
Sit still with your eyes closed, feeling your body rest against the
    chair.
Hold a precious object in your hands for more than two minutes.
Water some plants.
Empty trash from the house.

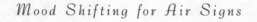

Mood Shifting for Air Signs

To increase clarity, concentration, or optimism:
Go outside and breathe in the air—night air is best.
Close your eyes and listen to your breathing for at least
    two minutes.
Take a whiff of fresh basil or rosemary.
Eat something peppermint.

To calm down or allay nervousness or confusion:
Sit in a quiet room for at least five minutes doing nothing.
Have a whiff of a favorite fragrance.
Knit, sew, or handle worry beads, loose change, or pebbles
    for at least five minutes.
Take a walk outside, concentrating on your feet feeling
    the ground beneath them.

Mood Shifting for Water Signs

**To open up emotions or
allow optimism, light, and flow:**

Splash some water on your face.

Boil some cinnamon.

Listen to some energetic music.

Take a deep breath and let it go with a shout, a yell, or by singing
loudly.

To calm, soothe, or diminish energy:

Drink some tea with honey.

Listen to calming music.

Say "Ah" with every exhale ten times.

Water the plants.

Spells for Holidays and Special Occasions

Spell for Successful Holidays (General)

Spell to Rekindle Christmas Spirit

Spell for Hanukkah

Spell to Welcome the New Year

Spell for Easter or Passover

Spell for Thanksgiving

Spell for St. Valentine's Day

Spell for Mother's Day

Spell for Father's Day

Spell for Reunions

Spell to Relieve a Holiday Hangover

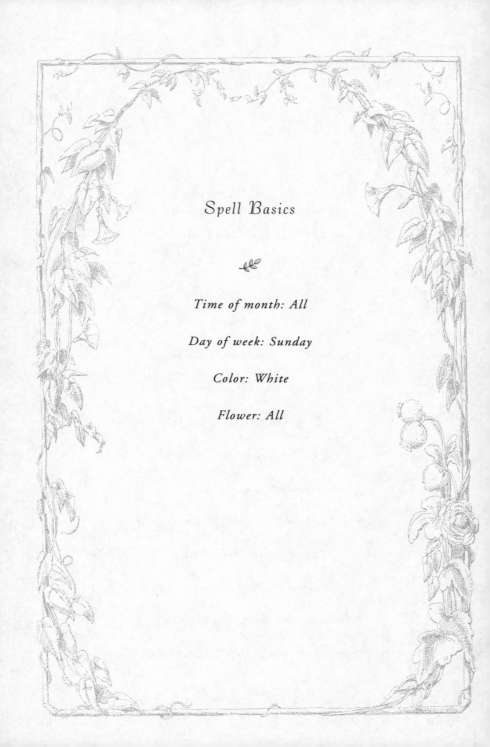

Spell Basics

꧁

Time of month: All

Day of week: Sunday

Color: White

Flower: All

*H*olidays and special occasions are often exercises in irony. We plan and look forward to each of them every year and then feel the beast of family tension, mishap, or just plain holiday letdown, never really enjoying them as much as we'd imagined we would. This isn't to say that everyone is disappointed at Christmastime or that every family turns into a psycho ward at a birthday party, but you know as well as I do that there are always opinions that don't mesh and attitudes that aren't in harmony whether or not they mess with the atmosphere. While spells aren't any substitute for therapy or family counseling, they certainly can help to make family occasions and special events into more agreeable experiences.

Tensions aren't the only thing that arise when holidays or occasions are on the calendar. The commercialization of holidays may have caused you to resist participating in an event altogether, or you may participate, but not very enthusiastically. Marketers capitalize on so many holidays—Mother's Day, St. Patrick's Day, the Fourth of July, just to name a few. I, for one, dreaded Father's Day because of the pressure of producing a present—on time and on target. Media overload can diminish your fun before it even starts.

In spite of the challenges, you can still salvage your own special occasions—whether they are sanctioned holidays or not—and turn them into affairs you'll remember with a smile. And spells can help.

Whatever the occasion, you can make it truly special, unique, and memorable when you put your heart into it. That doesn't mean working yourself to the bone to get your house clean and perfectly decorated or spending a week in the kitchen cooking. I'm talking about giving some thought to what you want from the day and putting some solid spiritual energy into it.

When you want to make something really special, start with your heart energy and go from there. Your heart's intention is what carries magic into your life. If you don't have any feeling for an occasion ("Oh no, it's time for our annual Fourth of July party, and I just don't feel up to it"), you might as well not have it. If your heart isn't in it, you won't enjoy yourself.

Conversely, if you put too much heart into your event, you can blast the life out of it and leave people feeling claustrophobic or stifled. Leave some creative space for magic to take place.

Creative Space in Special Occasions—A Must

One of my clients, Sherry, came to me for a recent consultation, ostensibly to have a business forecast but, as it turned out, really to discuss the fact that her son was coming home from college at Christmas and she wanted his stay at home to be perfect—a lot of quality family time balanced with time spent with his old high-school friends (of course, most college freshmen would tell you that the two are incompatible). Sherry had missed her son so much that she was tempted to "program" his time at home so that he would have to do something with her every day, from visiting grandparents to going to look at new computers. She also wanted to cook every single meal he had ever said he'd liked, and she wanted to just hang out with her son and husband on a "no plans" evening. Sherry was working herself into a state of agitation, already considering that her son would only be home for two weeks before leaving on a skiing trip (his Christmas present). She knew that she was going too far but couldn't find a way to let go. Sherry saw me only a week before her son was to arrive—and she was already dreading the day he would leave.

A bird's-eye view of this situation reveals classic holiday zeal that has nowhere to go but down. Overplanning, overprogramming, overeating is already in the works. Add to that trying to control how someone else feels (never a good idea) and then being depressed or let down even before you've had your fun. The most important element here is missing:

> ❧ *Coming together for a common purpose, be it to celebrate, honor, remember, or just reunite, presents a significant potential for group creativity that takes place without planning or foresight.*

The magic of any occasion is produced by the individuals who attend—not by the planner, cook, or host. While the people who make the event happen are of course important, no amount of food, candles, scent, or well-timed entertainment can make people enjoy themselves.

Sherry took a moment to consider this, and though it required a great deal of trust, she decided to let go and allow the universe to bring her what she craved most—special time with her son, which he would enjoy, too.

Spells come in very handy for special occasions, especially if your tendency is, like Sherry's, to not leave anything to chance. Sherry's story had a nice ending. Although her son grumped about having to see some relatives, he didn't complain about being overly burdened by his family. Also, Sherry left two days without any plans at all—no lunch or dinner, no activities. On one of these days her son disappeared with his friends until after midnight, but Sherry hung in there. On the other day without any plans, her son requested that they go to his favorite seafood restaurant and go shopping for a ski sweater. These mundane activities gave Sherry what she wanted—her son voluntarily spending time with her, talking to her about his life, and asking what she thought about things. The holiday itself was fine—Christmas dinner, family visits, all the trimmings—but this day was her greatest gift.

Sherry still has the tendency to go into overdrive when she knows her son is coming home, but she has worked out her formula for his visits to include some "no plan" time—to let things just happen.

SUCCESSFUL HOLIDAY MAGIC

Certain holidays, the "heavyweights," are worth discussing separately, since they are so jam-packed with importance, expectation, and media frenzy that it's hard to find their core energy. Christmas, Hanukkah, Kwanzaa, New Year's, Easter, Passover, and Thanksgiving are dense with expectation and can be quite tricky to pull off.

The key to your magic here is to use the core emotion of the holiday in your spell. This may be hard to define, but we'll take it one at a time.

CHRISTMAS

Christmas comes at a dark time, near the winter solstice, or shortest day of the year. While the key emotion for this occasion is joy and hope—celebrating the birth of a messenger of peace and love—it's hard to conjure bright cheerfulness while shadows grow long in the early afternoon. Melding the lightness of joy with the hibernation time of December suggests the need for a spell for loving family time, reconnection to what really is important in your lives, and a simple celebration of spiritual values. Using an Advent candle or calendar can be helpful, since it slowly brings attention to the coming of Christmas Eve. Going to Christmas services at church is like participating in a group spell and can reinforce the heart connection you probably want during this holiday.

Presents are fine—so is champagne and delicious food—but excessiveness is easily achieved during this time of year. Avoid burnout or overload with your personal spell for heart connection and blessing for Christmas.

Christmas Parties

Balancing elements and symbolism is inherent to a good party atmosphere. Your intention is important, but the way you create it is how the magic works. For instance, overkill occurs when there is just too much of the same theme or energy in one place. At a Christmas party, your own recipes and rituals will conjure an atmosphere that is right for you.

My friend Nancy throws a Christmas party every year. She plays in a band and has a lot of friends, so her hallmark is almost always music, singing, and lots of people. The first year of her Christmas party, she was still single and lived with girlfriends. They had a great tree, lots of food, and good music, but the high point of the party was when she insisted that we all sing "The Twelve Days of Christmas." As with most parties, a great many of the guests were standing in the kitchen (Vesta is popular even at Christmas), but Nancy, not to be ignored, got us to hold hands and sing. It took only a few minutes and the whole party was singing together (in shockingly bad harmony) the entire Christmas song. Now Nancy's parties always feature off-key singing, which takes place without her push. Both adults and children flock to her basement, where she has an entire band set up, with a microphone, of course, and it's one of the best and jolliest atmospheres I've ever experienced.

Nancy's party atmosphere reflects her energy, charm, and playfulness, and her guests respond in kind. Her party continues to be a Christmas tradition that her friends and family look forward to.

Your atmosphere will work best if it reflects your heart and intention. If something inspires you, go with it. If it doesn't, don't force it.

HANUKKAH

Hanukkah comes during the same dark time as Christmas and, ironically, the holiday stands for a "Miracle of Lights." Hanukkah commemorates a miracle that occurred after the destruction of the Great Temple in Jerusalem, when only a drop of oil remained for the menorah and was expected to keep it burning for just one day, but ended up keeping it burning for eight. This Jewish holiday easily gets swept along in the wake of Christmas to become a multidimensional gift-giving frenzy. It isn't hard to focus on the core of Hanukkah, however, since tradition dictates that candles be lit for each of its eight nights. The blessing recited with the lighting of the candles is much like a spell, although it lacks the water element.

To make Hanukkah more personal and bring in a little nonsectarian magic, you can thank Vesta for the fire in your home and the miracle of being warm, healthy, and together during this holiday, and raise a glass of wine or cider in celebration of miracles that happen every day.

KWANZAA

Kwanzaa, an African-American holiday created in 1966, is less commercialized than its neighbors, Christmas and Hanukkah. The celebration and rituals for Kwanzaa, which takes place from December 26 to January 1, focus on seven principles in seven days: unity, self-determination, collective work and responsibility, cooperative economics, purpose, creativity, and faith. Candles are lit every night, representing the principle of that day, and a ritual is performed during which various symbols of African heritage are placed on the table and everyone partakes in drinking from a "unity cup" as a way of strengthening the family and community. Kwanzaa uses every element needed for a spell.

The purpose of Kwanzaa is to reaffirm the culture and values of the African-American community. Because it is a dark time during which we stay inside with our families, winter—especially near the winter solstice on December 21—is an excellent time to reaffirm tradition and bonds. Kwanzaa makes the most of its season, and if its rituals are observed with heartfelt intention, they should prove to be a powerful spell themselves for love, creativity, and purposeful energy. Under these circumstances, there is no need to include any separate spells for Kwanzaa.

NEW YEAR'S EVE

Undoubtedly one of the most hyped holidays, New Year's Eve is like a holiday without a cause—it commemorates the end of a year based on our latest model of time (a Roman calendar that we have to adjust periodically). Even with the turn of a millennium, it's hard to find a cause or core to the event itself, and even with resolutions, there's not much to "do" unless you make your own ritual.

Since the new year is a time marker, it can serve as a turnover point, a time to let go of something (like a bad habit) or add something (like a good one) to your life. Unfortunately, the pressure to make a resolution is much greater than the incentive to see it through. Here's where a spell can help.

If you want to respect the new year as a "new energy," you can do a spell to turn over a new leaf and ask the universe to help you with it. Make it simple and don't put too much in the shopping cart—New Year's Eve isn't a particularly strong spell night unless it falls on a new moon.

If you're the type of person who cannot bear the idea of going to a party or celebrating at all, just skip this holiday and see it for what it is: December 31, just one day on the calendar.

EASTER AND PASSOVER

Both Easter and Passover are springtime celebrations with very sad backgrounds. Here's another holiday paradox: Like Christmas, which is a time of joy celebrated during a dark time of year, Easter and Passover are, at least in part, times of sadness celebrated during spring, a light time.

Christians mourn the death of Jesus on Good Friday and celebrate His resurrection on Easter Sunday. Death and rebirth. The Easter Bunny is more of a throwback to pagan times, when fertility rites were observed.

Jews retell the story of their ancestors' slavery under the Pharaoh and how Moses led them out of Egypt. Again, a bittersweet story.

This is not an easy time of year. Even though we like to think of pretty pastel colors, blooming flowers, and Easter egg hunts, there's real potential for confusion. Easter and Passover both have more somber sides that may not be acknowledged or observed directly, and this can cause a metaphysical hangover where no one feels quite right. Feelings of incompletion and anxiety are common.

A spell for a happy Easter or Passover needs to include some acknowledgment of the sadness, and a request for healing. This observance should be separate from the joyful, springtime activities associated with these holidays. If you go to church or conduct a Seder, you are acknowledging the heavier significance of these days, but even if you don't, you can acknowledge it by performing a spell.

THANKSGIVING

As children, we all heard the story about the Pilgrims and the first Thanksgiving. Nowadays most of us acknowledge that that was probably fabricated, and recognize that the basis for the holiday is an ancient harvest ritual. Thanksgiving is a time to express gratitude for the bounty of food, health, and prosperity that may have come to you during the year.

Although Thanksgiving heralds the official beginning of the Christmas buying season, it's a holiday that itself is virtually free of commercialization. Sure, turkey marketers and various food manufacturers try to make the most of the season, but Thanksgiving Day is basically a religion-free, hype-free family holiday, and, in being so, offers an excellent time for a spell to bring together your loved ones.

Whether or not you're all together under one roof on Thanksgiving Day makes no difference. Take some time to thank the universe for everything you count dear in your life. This ritual usually brings a deep sense of joy and a feeling of connection.

OTHER HOLIDAYS

There are a few other more minor holidays that you might want to celebrate with a spell. These are some of my favorites and can bring a nice energy to your household.

First, let's address Valentine's Day. Although this day isn't particularly old or powerful, St. Valentine's Day has become engrained as a marker of romantic love. I know of very few people—men or women—who feel happy to celebrate this day, for it more often than not reminds those of us who are without a mate that we're alone, and those of us who are with a mate that romantic moments come few and far between. Even schoolchildren get testy if they don't get a Valentine from someone they like. The broad commercialization of this holiday makes it almost impossible to avoid, and so it's an irritation.

To celebrate St. Valentine's Day, do a spell for love. Whether you are eight or eighty, it's always nice to cast a spell that brings love back into your life, increases the love you already have, or at least deepens your connection to it. The holiday itself, although it means nothing, does cast a lot of current psychic energy on the day, which makes it a powerful time to cast that spell. You won't regret it and it can't hurt.

MOTHER'S DAY AND FATHER'S DAY

It is very hard for many to get revved up for these modern, merchandised holidays. The pressure to get the "right" present, do something touching and meaningful, is too much. The right thing to do on this kind of holiday is simply to cast a spell (before the day) and ask that the day be special for the person you want to honor. If you are inclined to make dinner, go out for lunch, take a walk in the park, or just let that poor tired parent have a day to themselves, do so. Your "gift" should be what you want to give, not what you think you have to.

REUNIONS

Bearing in mind that these aren't real holidays, still they are certainly special occasions and can send the most even-tempered individual into a snit. Reunions are often chock-full of anticipation but result in some mild shock and letdown.

You've heard that "you can't go home again," but most of us will attempt to re-create a time when the group was together and, of course, younger. Family reunions, high-school or college reunions, even work reunions force groups to look back and find common threads—even if those threads have become unraveled.

If you play host to a reunion or are merely attending one, be sure to cast a spell for spaciousness and reconnection so that you can avoid being pegged back into the past. You can at least conjure an experience that won't force you into a time warp, and you may even be entertained by the results.

SAD OCCASIONS

The hardest atmospheres to conjure are for somber occasions, like after funerals or memorial services. These can be very awkward for both host and guest. Rather than lean into a "funereal atmosphere," try conjuring energy for healing.

Funerals bring people together in the same way weddings do, except for the fact that with funerals the occasion is sad. The reunion quality of the gathering can be disconcerting to the bereaved, but that's a reality of the occasion. Still, there are bound to be hugs and smiles amid the sadness, and usually someone will have to laugh or toss off a few jokes to ease the discomfort with death. All of this behavior is normal.

These somber get-togethers benefit from supportive, loving, gentle energy so that the many emotions guests may experience are allowed to surface.

Things to Help Conjure a Healing Atmosphere

White candles burning (fire)
Crystals hanging in windows or near lamps to catch light (air)
Discreetly placed tissue boxes (earth/water)
The fragrance of baking bread or roasting meat (air)
Photo albums with pictures of happy times with the deceased (earth)
A room for children to play in, separate from the main room (earth)
Plants (earth)
Soft classical music or jazz for background (water)

Things to Avoid

Too many flowers or candles
Somber music
Cold rooms
Incense

Healing atmospheres combine the purpose of the occasion with gentle reminders of coziness, prosperity, and life-affirming presence.

For instance, white candles represent healing and spiritual energy. Crystals, especially when they refract light, reinforce spiritual energy and enhance well-being. Tissues must be at hand for anyone who might be moved to tears, so that they will not be embarrassed. Fragrances from the kitchen (smells of bread or a meal cooking) are very nurturing. Plants are subtly life-affirming without the funereal association that flowers can bring, and soft background music lends gentle emotional support. There are two reasons why children need a separate room to play in: First, it allows them to be themselves when they want to let off steam, without annoying their parents or guests, and second, it gives adults a place to go if they want a breath of life. Children can be very healing, especially when death is at hand.

HOLIDAY HANGOVERS

Every year we watch the joyful buildup of Christmas with decorations, cooking, gift buying, and anticipation. Then it's over. Boom. Abruptly, all that joviality, excitement, and eagerness is gone and we're left with old trees, empty streets, and early-evening darkness. Christmas yields big holiday hangovers for almost everyone, but it's not the only time you might feel down after a holiday. Any event that includes some buildup and anticipation and holds a special date on your calendar can give way to letdown after it's over.

The atmosphere of letdown is quite a drag on everyone. As with cleaning up after a party when the guests have gone home, you're left with remnants of a good time and the harsh finality that it's over. These atmospheres have to happen—there's no avoiding them—but you can shift them very soon if you want to. No sense lolling around in depression if you don't have to.

Gary, one of my clients, always kicks back after Christmas and lets his cats and kids play in discarded wrapping paper, boxes, and ribbons for the next couple of days. Then, on the twenty-eighth, he gives everyone trash bags and the whole family cleans the house of Christmas stuff, including the tree, its ornaments, and the outdoor decorations. While his neighbors leave lights up for another week or two, Gary gets his house together for the new year, all clean, tidy, and ready for January. He tackles his post-Christmas blues by his drive for order, and when the chores are done, he gets the whole family to help make dinner, each dictating a favorite dish to include in the menu. He also gives his kids what he calls "Director's Night," where each child gets a night to pick out a movie for the family to watch.

Gary's way of dealing with a holiday hangover is effective—he uses a group cleaning effort to shift the atmosphere, and makes the most of his time with his family by doing indoor, family-geared activities that keep the fires of Vesta burning brightly.

If you suffer from holiday hangovers, create your own rituals and try a spell for releasing the holiday energy that may be keeping you from moving on.

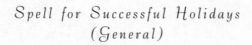

Spell for Successful Holidays
(General)

On a Sunday during a waxing moon
and in the third hour after sunset,
light a white candle.
Place white flowers in a vase with water.

Say aloud:
I ask guardians and guides,
god and goddess to join with
me in blessing the upcoming holiday.
I anchor your sacred energy on that day
to benefit all who join in its observance.
I ask that the day goes smoothly into night,
that hearts are calm and joined in purpose,
and that all who attend participate in spirit
for the greater good of all.
I affirm this is done for the greater good and
say,
So be it.
And so it is.

Blow out the candle.
Relight it on the holiday.

Spell to Rekindle Christmas Spirit

On a Sunday prior to Christmas
and in the first hour after sunset,
light a red candle and a green candle.
Place some evergreens in a vase with water
(or you can use your Christmas tree).
Place an object that reminds you of the spirit
of Christmas next to the candles.

Say aloud:
*I call in the great spirit of god
and all the good spirit manifests to
anchor and protect the spirit of Christmas.
I affirm that I celebrate the birth of Christ
and His message of peace, forgiveness, and love.
I ask that all who celebrate and observe this
day with me and my family feel
touched by the energy and power of Christ's birth
and that our lives participate in our connection to
His message in the year to come.
I ask that the heart of Christmas be strong, pure, and true.
So be it.
And so it is.*

Blow out the candles.
Relight them for your Christmas celebration.

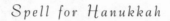

Spell for Hanukkah

On a Sunday prior to Hanukkah
and in the first hour after sunset,
light a blue candle and a white candle.
Place some flowers in a vase with water.

Say aloud:
*I gather in the spirit of the
Maccabees, guides, prophets, and memories
of all who came before me, to conjure
the energy of wonder and celebration over the
miracle of lights.
I ask that all who come and observe this holiday
be touched by its meaning,
that all souls be open to miracles of spirit,
faith, and trust.
I ask that this be done for the greater good of all
and for the continued legacy of commemoration.
So be it.
And so it is.*

Blow out the candles.
Use them for your Hanukkah celebrations.

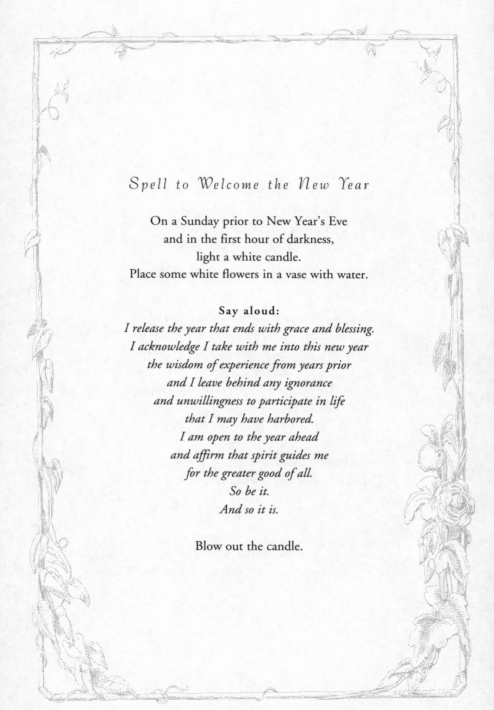

Spell to Welcome the New Year

On a Sunday prior to New Year's Eve
and in the first hour of darkness,
light a white candle.
Place some white flowers in a vase with water.

Say aloud:
I release the year that ends with grace and blessing.
I acknowledge I take with me into this new year
the wisdom of experience from years prior
and I leave behind any ignorance
and unwillingness to participate in life
that I may have harbored.
I am open to the year ahead
and affirm that spirit guides me
for the greater good of all.
So be it.
And so it is.

Blow out the candle.

Spell for Easter or Passover

On a Sunday prior to Easter or Passover
and in the first hour of darkness,
light a white candle.
Place some spring flowers in a vase with water.
Place some ice in a bowl made of organic materials.

Say aloud:

*I gather in the spirit of my ancestors,
of god, goddess, and all those who guide
both heaven and earth,
to acknowledge the coming of spring and
the solemn commemoration of this time.
With death there is rebirth,
with life there is death.
I participate in this cycle of god's will
with faith and trust.
As this ice melts, so does the sorrow of loss,
and as these flowers fade, so does the vitality of life.
I ask that this time be marked with respect for
both life and death, mystery and miracle.
For the greater good, I say,
So be it.
And so it is.*

Blow out the candle.
Let the ice melt (about a day) and
add the water to the flowers.

Spell for Thanksgiving

After sunset on the Sunday prior to Thanksgiving,
light a white candle and a gold or orange candle.
Place a bowl of autumn fruit next to the candle.
Put some fall flowers in a vase with water.

Say aloud:
*I bless the coming Thanksgiving holiday
and ask that spirit endow our celebration
with the true heart of gratitude.
I affirm that we are all appreciative of the health,
wealth, and joy we have shared in this year
and ask that we may benefit from our work once again.
I ask that all those who attend this observance
feel the light of gratitude and that this energy
contribute to the greater good of all.
With respect for the miracle of everyday life
and for the bounty of our harvest, I say,
So be it.
And so it is.*

Blow out the candles. Relight them for the holiday.
Place the bowl of fruit out at your Thanksgiving celebration
and allow your guests to eat freely from it.

Spell for St. Valentine's Day

On a Sunday before Valentine's Day and in the
fourth hour after sunset,
light a pink candle and a white candle.
Place some pink flowers in a vase with water.
Place a memento or photo of a loved one next to the candle.

Say aloud:
*I call upon St. Valentine and the spirit of
love in anticipation of Valentine's Day
and ask that this observance
be filled with love, gentle joy, and heart's ease.
I affirm that there is love in my life and that
I am open to all love, that I willingly
share love and participate in love's play.
I respect the holiday as a day
to open my heart in all ways and to
allow the flow of love to come to me throughout
the year and with the magic of the universe.
I ask that this be done for the greater good of all.
So be it.
And so it is.*

Blow out the candles.
Light the candles on St. Valentine's Day once again.

Spell for Mother's Day

On the Sunday before or the Sunday of Mother's Day
and in the first hour after sunset,
light a white candle and a pink candle.
Place spring flowers in a vase with water.
Place a photo or object related to your mother or grandmother
next to the flowers.

Say aloud:

On this day of blessing and healing,
I affirm my love and respect for the
miracle of birth and nurturing,
and offer thanks and respect
to my mother.
I ask Vesta, Venus, and all mother
goddesses of ancient time to join with me and with spirit
today to honor the energy, time, and life force
given to me by my mother, her mother,
and the mothers before her.
I am grateful for the blessing of life and
for the love, wisdom, and care I have received.
With this, I honor my mother.
May blessings and healing be with her.
So be it.
And so it is.

Let the candles burn as long as you like.
Set them aside to use for healing spells or
for Father's Day. Offer the flowers to your
mother or keep them next to her photo.

Spell for Father's Day

On the Sunday before or the Sunday of Father's Day
and in the first hour after sunset,
light a pink candle and a white candle.
Place summer flowers in a vase
and place a photo of your father or an object
related to him next to the candles.

Say aloud:
*On this day of blessing and healing,
I affirm my love and respect for the
miracle of birth and protection,
and offer thanks and respect
to my father.
I ask that all ancient gods and rulers of fatherhood
join with me and with spirit
today to honor the energy, time, and life force
given to me by my father, his father,
and the fathers before him.
I am grateful for the blessing of life and
for the love, power, and protection I have received.
With this, I honor my father.
May blessings and healing be with him.
So be it.
And so it is.*

Let the candles burn as long as you like.
Set them aside to use for healing spells or
for the next Mother's Day. Offer the flowers to your
father or keep them next to his photo.

Spell for Reunions

On a Thursday during a waxing moon and
in the second hour after sunset,
light a blue candle and a pink candle.
Place some lavender in a vessel made with organic
materials. Place some oil or liquid scent of vanilla
open next to the lavender.

Say aloud:
*I call in the forces of nature and of man
and ask them to join with me to conjure
a warm and gentle reunion of hearts and minds.
I ask that the day of _____ be blessed
with the energy of connection, clarity, lightness,
and spaciousness to accommodate all those beings
who attend this gathering.
I affirm that I am open to the day and participate
in the energy of reuniting with a group that was once
close, and I ask that the energy of the past weave
lightly through our lives of the present,
so that we remember, honor, and enjoy all that has
come before and all that may now ensue.
I ask that this be done for the greater good
of all, and say,
So be it.
And so it is.*

Blow out the candles. If you can, bring them
to the reunion and relight them. Carry some
of the lavender on your person, and dab some
vanilla scent on your solar plexus while dressing
for the reunion.

Spell to Relieve a Holiday Hangover

On the day after the holiday or on a Saturday
in the first hour after sunset,
light a white candle.
Place flowers or plants left over from the occasion
next to the candle.
Place a glass of water and a pack of matches next to them.

Say aloud:
*We mark the end of this holiday with
quiet resolve and gently release the energy
of anticipation from our atmosphere.
We thank spirit for bringing us this time of
healthy celebration and release our hold over
this much-loved time of year.
As we let go, we cleanse, making room for what is to come.
We gently wash what is left from the past
[take some water on your fingertips and shake it off]
and purify our home that we may be open to our future
[light a match and blow it out].*

*With the power of fire, earth, air, and water
we work and live in harmony.
This release is gentle,
this healing is complete.
So be it.
And so it is.*

Throw out the flowers or plants
when they start to die.

Nature's Harmony in Your Home

Spell for the Winter Solstice (December 21)

Spell for Candlemas (February 1)

Spell for the Vernal (Spring) Equinox (March 21)

Spell for May Day (May 1)

Spell for the Summer Solstice (June 21)

Spell for Lammas (August 1)

Spell for the Autumnal Equinox (September 21)

Spell for Halloween (October 31)

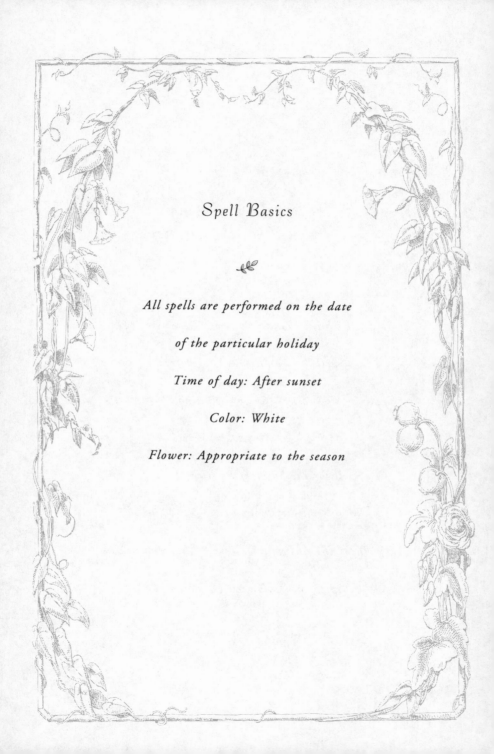

Spell Basics

All spells are performed on the date

of the particular holiday

Time of day: After sunset

Color: White

Flower: Appropriate to the season

Wherever you live, your home is situated in what used to be land claimed by nature. Your home may stand where there was once forest, or swamp, or prairie. Even though you may live in a paved environment today, the ground beneath that surface is nature's turf. It's easy to forget that nature is at the bottom of all of our dwellings. Moreover, large buildings, even the mightiest fortress, can fall to ruins from nature's relentless power and become little more than a mound overtaken by growth.

Left to its own course, nature will intrude on your home—tree roots in your sewage system, ivy growing onto windows—but assuming that you keep up on your home's maintenance and you aren't subjected to hurricanes or tornadoes or floods on a constant basis, you're probably not going to be reminded of nature's more fearful force very often. The destructive character of Mother Nature is not an issue in this book; instead, I want you to focus on the gentle guidance and support nature can provide for your home through simple acts of respect.

Long ago, people were much more connected to nature and could predict weather, crop seasons, and more just from observing the countryside. Cows grouped together on a hillside foretold rain; a sharp horizon line at dusk meant bad weather to come. But very few of us are fortunate enough to witness cows on a daily basis, and an unblemished horizon line is very hard to come by. We also have heating in the winter and air-conditioning in the summer to keep us in comfort, and electric lights to keep us going even when the sun sets early. We are actually quite divorced from nature's energy in our daily lives and may be adversely affected as a result.

By showing respect for nature on a regular basis and using its energy skillfully, you can make your home safer, more welcoming, supportive, and comfortable, and you will be more conscious of shifts, movements, or other gentle nudges that nature provides to help you along in life.

You may be fortunate enough to have a garden, which will keep you fairly apprised of nature's cycles and energy shifts, or you may just have a few indoor plants or a window box. In either case, participating in plant life helps to reconnect you to nature.

YOUR GARDEN—INDOORS AND OUT

If you can plant your own garden and design the landscape surrounding your house, you are both fortunate and probably busy, for a garden demands attention year-round to be at its best. Gardens are such special places, constantly responding to natural forces and producing growth and harvest every year. Your garden might be just two tulip bulbs in a pot on your terrace, or several plots planted carefully with herbs, flowers, and vegetables. As long as you tend a garden, you are hooking up to the magical force of nature.

Taking care of a garden or plants demands that you nurture (by watering, weeding, or harvesting) and participate in natural life cycles. Once you find the groove of nature's cycle, you can apply it to your own life and the lives of your family members. This makes your household more at peace with outer, natural forces and certainly more alive and in sync with nature's power. The benefits of tending to plants are worth the time you put into it.

Every tree, plant, shrub, and flower emits an energy and personality of its own. Most of their "characters" have been assigned powers or symbolic meaning over thousands of years. Some plants offer real medicinal qualities, like aloe; others are decorative or fragrant, like flowers; while still others are symbolic, like the oak tree. These symbolic meanings are actually very powerful. Even if you don't know off the top of your head what an evergreen tree, for example, symbolizes, your unconscious or intuitive faculty will probably know that the tree stands for long life or immortality.

If you know what kind of plants and trees surround your home, you can look up their meaning and see how they influence your home's outer energy.

If you have the opportunity to design your own garden, you might want to consider using some of the plants listed here. You'll be able to use them in spells and in adding some nice magical energy to your environs.

If you live in a city or in a place where you don't have a garden, use this information to collect things from nature to keep in your house or apartment, like an acorn from an oak tree or a collection of pinecones or autumn leaves. It's not that an acorn has the same energy as an old oak tree, but it's better than living without that energy at all.

Trees

Trees have traditionally been a symbol of life—for their fruits and protection from the elements—and of wisdom—for their long lives and what they must witness over the years. Below are common tree types and magical properties or symbols associated with them or their fruits or seeds.

Tree	Symbolism
Acacia	Sacred energy, purity
Almond	Prosperity
Apple	Love, garden magic
Apricot	Love
Ash	Unlocks magic
Aspen	Protection against theft
Bamboo	Luck
Banyan	Luck
Beech	Wishes, creative powers
Birch	Purification
Bodhi	Meditation, wisdom, protection
Cactus	Protection, chastity
Cedar	Welcomes positive energy
Cherry	Virginity
Chestnut	Love, fertility
Cypress	Death and rebirth
Dogwood	Wishes, protection
Ebony	Protection, power
Elder	Protection, wards off evil
Elm	Love, feminine powers
Eucalyptus	Healing
Fig	Divination, fertility
Fir	Long life
Hawthorn	Fertility
Maple	Love, money
Mesquite	Healing
Oak	Dignity, wisdom
Olive	Healing, peace, potency
Orange	Love, luck

Palm, date	Fertility
Peach	Love, protection
Pear	Lust
Pecan	Money
Pine	Immortality, fertility
Plum	Love, protection
Poplar	Money
Rowan	Psychic powers, magic
Sandalwood	Protection, wisdom, spirituality
Sycamore	Feminine power, protection of the dead
Walnut	Health
Willow	Mourning, protection
Yew	Raising the dead

flowers

If you're planting a flower garden or have flowers growing nearby, check out their symbolic properties. Here are a few selected flowers and their magical or mythical significance. You're sure to use some of these flowers in performing your spells. Growing your own spell ingredients only strengthens your magic, so you might consider raising a little rose plant (I have one on my windowsill) or planting a tulip bulb for spring. Many flowers are now made to grow indoors as well as outside.

Flower	Symbolism
African violet	Protection
Amaranth	Immortality
Anemone	Fertility
Bluebell	Luck
Columbine	Love, protection
Daffodil	Success

Daisy	Love
Dandelion	Divination
Gardenia	Love
Geranium	Courage
Hibiscus	Divination
Hyacinth	Love, lust
Hydrangea	Breaks hexes
Iris	Feminine protection
Lilac	Harmony
Lily	Virginity
Lily of the valley	Mental powers
Marigold	Psychic powers
Morning glory	Harmony
Narcissus	Beauty, love
Orchid	Fertility, seduction
Pansy	Thoughtfulness
Peony	Illumination
Poppy	Transformation
Primrose	Protection
Rose	Love
Sunflower	Success, fertility
Tulip	Prosperity
Violet	Love

General Plants and Herbs

There are so many plants in our world that I cannot even attempt to catalog them all with their magical powers and symbolism. I will, however, give you a very brief list of common plants and herbs and their properties. If you want more information, you can consult one of the many useful books devoted to this subject (I recommend *Cunning-*

ham's Encyclopedia of Magical Herbs). The following compilation comes from several sources as well as my own research and experience.

Plants and Herbs	Symbolism
Arum	Sexuality
Basil	Love, wealth, peace
Bergamot	Money
Borage	Courage
Caraway	Protection against evil
Catnip	Love
Chamomile	Money
Coriander	Health
Dill	Protection, wealth
Fennel	Protection against fire
Fern	Protection
Foxglove	Fairy magic, garden protection
Grass	Triumph
Hemp	Magic
Ivy	Protection
Juniper	Protection against theft
Lavender	Love, friendship
Lovage	Love
Marjoram	Happiness
Mint	Money
Mistletoe	Love
Parsley	Lust
Rosemary	Purification
Sage	Wisdom, longevity
Thyme	Health and healing
Verbena	Love

As you have seen, there are many options for you to choose from if you are growing your own garden, and even if you are limited to indoor plants, you can still grow quite a few different "energies." Just to get you started, here are some suggestions for what you can include in your indoor and outdoor gardens.

Outdoor Gardens

Shady or Limited Sun Garden
Ivy (protection)
Lily of the valley (mental powers)
Parsley (lust)
Violets (love)

Dry Gardens
Borage (courage)
Chamomile (money)
Daisies (love)
Fennel (protection against fire)
Lavender (love and friendship)
Rosemary (purification)
Sage (wisdom and longevity)
Thyme (health and healing)

Moist Gardens
Bergamot (money)
Lovage (love)
Mint (money)
Parsley (lust)
Poppy (transformation)
Primrose (protection)
Violets (love)

These are only a few suggestions to get you thinking about what you can plant outside of your home. Don't be daunted by your soil or by weather conditions, for there are many ways to get nature to cooperate with your planting ambitions. If you want to get really serious, buy a book on gardening that has a magical twist to it, which will help you create a really special, powerful place in which you can meditate, heal, and create the basics for most of your spells.

Indoor Gardens

An apartment dweller myself, I am continually trying to bring life into our household. Though it used to be limited to houseplants, today indoor gardening has become more creative and, happily, more magic-friendly. You can grow many herbs inside or on the window ledge of your home. Here are some suggestions to get you started. If you doubt your capacity to really nurture and care for a plant, start with only one or two and move on from there. Failure is easy if you get too ambitious. And finally, don't be dispirited if your plants die. They have their own life cycle and it's okay for them to go.

Indoor Herbs

Basil (love, wealth, peace)
Borage (courage)
Dill (protection, wealth)
Lavender (love and friendship)
Marjoram (happiness)
Mint (money)
Parsley (lust)
Rosemary (protection)
Sage (wisdom, longevity)
Thyme (health and healing)
Verbena (love)

Now that I've got you participating in some sort of plant-tending, you are ready to be witness to the real magic of nature's power. You will see that natural phases in our year are much more obvious when you see a simple plant's reaction. There are eight significant natural time points during our calendar year that mark a shift in nature's energy and in our own physical and emotional responses. Keep an eye on your plants on each of these time points and sense how you might be feeling, too. These ancient time points were important "holidays" thousands of years ago; now most of them have faded or are replaced by modern versions.

Winter solstice	December 21
Candlemas	February 1
Spring equinox	March 21
May Day	May 1
Summer solstice	June 21
Lammas	August 1
Autumnal equinox	September 21
Halloween	October 31

Winter Solstice

The cycle starts with the winter solstice, which is the simultaneous death and rebirth of the sun's presence on our planet. This day is the shortest of the year, and the ancients built extremely precise structures to celebrate this particular moment, like Stonehenge in England and Newgrange in Ireland. Both of these mysterious stone monuments celebrate the sun's position on the day of the solstice, usually the twenty-first of December.

In my experience, this is the single most powerful day of the year, and is particularly good for casting spells. It is the day of greatest darkness, and hence has the greatest potential for magic. Winter is introduced by the solstice, a season of fear and quiet, internal rather than external energy. Animals hibernate—we all want to sleep more—and gardens lie dormant. This day is rich in its power to release the passing cycle and to dream of, conjure, and create the next cycle. The winter solstice is the New Year's Eve of nature.

My clients know and respect this time point more than any other, and many of them have seen fruits from their solstice spells during the following year. Although this isn't a lighthearted party time, some people conduct group solstice celebrations at which they congregate to do the spell together. Since group power is very potent, I encourage these gatherings.

Candlemas

Six weeks later, just around the time we are all looking for the groundhog's reaction to his shadow, there is another natural time point. This is a lovely old holiday once called Imbolc but more commonly known today as Candlemas; it is still celebrated by some religions. The natural significance of Candlemas is the turning toward light; February 1 marks the day that the darkest six weeks of winter are past and the next six weeks will bring more and more daylight.

Generally at this time you can find the beginnings of life in a garden again—even in harsh climates, snowdrops or a crocus can break through. There may also be a thaw or slight breeze that whispers spring—just enough to wake you up from the sleepy, slow time of winter.

Candlemas is celebrated with lots of candles, to illuminate the darkness and welcome back returning warmth and light. I contend that this lovely time point needs to be observed more often; doing so will result in a soothing and beautiful energy in your home.

Vernal (Spring) Equinox

Both Easter and Passover tend to fall around the spring equinox, which, like the holidays themselves, celebrates rebirth. Marking a new season, the equinox is the point at which light overtakes darkness, daylight predominates over night, and the energy of the growing season begins.

The equinox is the balance of sun and darkness, but by this time we are so ready to be done with winter that the observance of spring takes on a tonality that emphasizes the light. A ritual planting is a significant way to respect the equinox. I grew a six-foot sunflower from a seed that was planted in my apartment on the spring equinox, and I've grown many other kinds of plants from seeds as well, but it's not necessary to grow the plant to fruition, it's important just that you plant *something*. The time to initiate is now, and planting a seed is a symbolic gesture of beginning to participate in nature's growing cycle.

May Day

While May Day is a laborer's holiday in Eastern Europe, not much is known about its roots. May Day, also known as Beltane, is the holiday the ancients might have called "Sex, Drugs, and Rock and Roll." May Day marks a fertile, giddy time when love, lust, and joyful celebrations take place to honor the potential of the earth to produce a harvest. The weather is usually good, hopes are often high, and it's easy and agreeable to spend time outside.

Celebrating May Day a thousand years ago might have been more bacchanalian than we approve of, with drinking and potent herbs inducing states of euphoria, fires burning in the countryside all night to keep revelers lively, and some playful sexuality in respect of Mother Nature, whose land is fertile and ready to give birth to crops. While this kind of observance may seem tempting, I don't necessarily recommend it today.

Rather, the May Day time point is simply a time to be in your garden and enjoy the growing opportunities around you and your family. You may want to eat outside, let go of work and just enjoy the evening.

Summer Solstice

At the halfway point, the summer solstice, daylight reaches its maximum and we have the longest day of the year. Like the winter solstice, it's a time of endings and beginnings. Spring gives way to summer, light gives way to dark.

Although daylight will now begin to be lost little by little, the summer solstice time point is primarily a time of joy. Usually the work in a garden, the preparation and planting of vegetables and fruits, is done by now. It's time to weed and wait for the harvest. Summer is slightly idle, slow and easy, and is fallow like winter, but rather than fear, summer brings joy.

Because it's a very light time, the summer solstice is not a strong time for magic. While you can still cast effective spells, you won't feel compelled to undertake great cosmic projects, since summer energy is about working on the harvest and making it real.

Lammas

Of all the time points we're mentioning, this one has endured the least into our modern age. Lammas marks the midpoint of summer, around August 1, when the first harvest is made. If you're fortunate enough to be in the country, look for the signs, like rolled bales of hay or farm equipment slowing traffic down.

Ancients observed this time point with loaves of bread made from the first harvest. Because it's the midpoint of summer, it's probably very hot and is often time for vacations. Farm workers are just gearing up to reap the bounty of the year's planting, and it's a good time for you to look at your plantings and decide when your harvest or peak growth will be reached.

The observance of Lammas is not an active or hard-working one. Rather, it's a time to indulge in the last of summer's slow, meandering energy before the work of the autumn starts in earnest.

Autumnal Equinox

On September 21, autumn is introduced by another balancing of day and night hours as the sun gives way to the increasing shadow time. Darkness is about to overtake daylight.

The more passive energy of summer is over; hard work takes over to harvest, reap, and reward the year's efforts. This equinox is a checkpoint at which to see what has transpired in your life since that dark winter solstice and how far you've come since spring's plantings.

In general, this is a time point of gratitude for the harvest and blessing for the coming shadow time. Ancient cultures celebrated bounty and at the same time observed that the shadow time, one that could bring bad weather, sickness, and scarcity, was coming soon. This equinox can have a more sobering energy than its spring counterpart.

Halloween

On October 31, the United States observes an aberration of the ancient holiday of Halloween, the venerable time point called Samhain. Samhain respects death. The harvest is over, gardens lie fallow, weather has become colder, harsher, and challenging. The midpoint of autumn is passing, and the earth is "dying" into winter.

Halloween is an extremely powerful marker, second only to the winter solstice for its magic potential. Spells and blessings are strong on this day, since it is a time when the realms are closest. The night of Halloween really is a time for the dead to speak to us, but not to spook or scare us.

This ancient holiday parallels the earth's life cycle—now the ground is fallow, plants have died, leaves have fallen from trees. The "death" of the earth is upon us, and so it is time to remember our ancestors and the spirits who protect us and guide us. Halloween is an excellent time to send messages to and receive messages from those who have passed on, as well as a time to ask for help in conjuring and bringing spells to fruition.

While "trick or treat" is very nice for children, adults should observe this time point with respect. If you have a jack-o'-lantern, you can perform a simple spell just by lighting its candle for loved ones who are gone. There is a somber side to this commercial ghoul-and-candy holiday, and you can bring a strong energy of blessing and protection into your home by observing it.

Spell for the Winter Solstice
(December 21)

Make a list of everything you wish to manifest during the
next year, including what you wish for your family and other
loved ones.
Be complete—include things related to career, relationships,
health, and other factors like clarity, confidence, and fun.
After sunset, light a white candle.
Place a vase of flowers you like next to the candle.

Say aloud:
*I gather in the power of mystery and creation.
Of goddess and god, yin and yang.
I call in the elements,
fire, earth, air, and water,
to work with me to manifest my desires in the coming cycle.*

Read your list aloud.

Say aloud:
*I affirm that I am able and willing to allow these wishes
to manifest for the greater good of all
and that I participate
in the energy of creation, nurturing, and harvest.
So be it.
And so it is.*

Allow the candle to burn until you go to sleep.
Save your list by putting it somewhere safe.
Respect the evening by drinking or
eating something special.

Spell for Candlemas (February 1)

After sunset,
light as many candles as you can, placing
them all around the room.
Place a vase with orange, yellow, or red flowers
somewhere in the room.
Sit in the candlelight,
breathing in the warmth, light, and color.

Say aloud:
*On this precious eve,
when the time is still winter
but spring whispers its coming,
we slowly welcome back the light of the sun.
While we finish our rest and the
earth prepares to wake from its cold slumber,
we turn to the sky and see
the fire of the sun growing in power.
As this magic time of darkness recedes and we sit
with the joy of stillness,
may the warmth of these flames
enkindle joy and hope in the hearts of all beings
that the healing of winter is nearing its end,
the life of the garden
is creeping quietly back to life.
The glow of our candles welcomes back the light.
So be it.
And so it is.*

Enjoy your evening by candlelight.

Spell for the Vernal (Spring) Equinox (March 21)*

Make a list of everything you wish to manifest
between now and December 21 (or use the list you made on
the last winter solstice).
Light a green candle and a candle of your favorite color.
Place a vase of spring flowers next to the candles.
Place a plant and a glass of water alongside the flowers.

Say aloud:
*I call in the forces
of the elements, fire, earth, air, and water,
on this eve of rebirth.
May god and goddess join with
me to create and manifest
these heart's desires.*

Read your list aloud.

Say aloud:

*I honor the guardians and know that
this work rests in their mystery.
I claim my power consciously and
express it within the greater good.
I allow compassion, temperance, and gratitude
to guide me in this journey.
And, with the forces around me, I release this with
love, faith, and trust and say,
So be it.
And so it is.*

Water the plant.
Let the candles burn as long as you like.
This spell may be repeated during a waxing moon
on any day of the week until June 21, 2000.

*To be performed on the evening of the vernal (spring) equinox.

Spell for May Day (May 1)

After sunset,
light a yellow candle.
Place spring flowers in a vase with water
or perform your spell outside.
Place a glass of wine or juice
and something sweet to eat before the candle.

Say aloud:

On this evening of great goddess power,
I participate in the forces of nature
and the creative energy of the elements
to celebrate the joy of the fertile growing season.
By day I do the work of spirit
in love, life, creativity, and nurturing,
and this night I put aside work to enjoy
the mystery and delight of physical being.
I play with, gaze upon, and imagine
all the beauty and pleasure this world holds.
I rest in my faith and heart in the knowledge that
this magical day endows growth, hope, light, and healing
to all beings in need.
I ask that this be done for the greater good of all.
So be it.
And so it is.

Let the candle burn as long as you like.
Eat, drink, and enjoy yourself with others.

Spell for the Summer Solstice
(June 21)

Make a list of everything you wish to manifest
during the next six months (or use the list you made on the
last winter solstice).
Be complete—include things related to career, personal issues,
and other factors like clarity, confidence, and fun.
After sunset (around eight-thirty),
light a candle of your choice.
Place a vase of flowers you like next to the candle.

Say aloud:
*I gather in the power of this day of greatest light
and call in the guardians of fire, earth, air, and water
to bring the last grace of power in light to
manifest my desires in the coming harvest.
I ask that this be done within the greater good.*

Read your list aloud.

Say aloud:
*I affirm that I am able and willing to allow these wishes
to manifest and I participate in the miracle of creation
and with faith.
So be it.
And so it is.*

Allow the candle to burn until you go to sleep.
Celebrate the energy of the evening in some way—
play music, raise a glass, allow yourself some indulgence.

Spell for Lammas (August 1)

After sunset,
light a gold or orange candle.
Place a loaf of bread
and some grape juice or wine
next to the candle.
Perform this spell outside if possible.

Say aloud:
*On this golden evening,
in the waning energy of summer's light,
I raise my glass to greet the harvest
and prepare to do the work of this cycle.
Under the guidance of the elements
and with the grace of spirit,
I take to this task with quiet purpose,
faith, and a dedicated heart.
I accept what the growing shadow brings
and I open to the mystery of creation,
as the earth gives birth to our harvest.
As the sun's heat gives way to autumn's frost,
so does the light give way to dark.
May this crop of wheat be plentiful
and may the vines bear sweet and healthy wines.
Whatever we reap, may we have faith in the universe.
So be it.
And so it is.*

Eat a slice of bread.
Drink some wine or juice.
Enjoy a quiet evening.

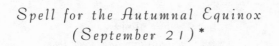

Spell for the Autumnal Equinox
(September 21) *

Take the list of all you wished to have manifested this year
(before December 21) and read it aloud.
If you did not make this list at the last equinox (vernal),
then make a list now of things that have manifested
or are manifesting for you at this time. Do not
list long-term goals at this time. Read this list aloud.
Light a green candle and a yellow or orange candle.
Place a vase of autumn flowers next to the candles.
Place an apple (from the new harvest) next to the flowers.

Say aloud:
I call in the forces
of the elements on this eve of the harvest.
May god and goddess join with
me to bless the manifestation of
all my heart's desires.

Read your list aloud.

Say aloud:
I honor the guardians and know that
this work rests in their mystery.
I claim my power consciously and
express it within the greater good.
I allow compassion, temperance, and gratitude
to guide me in this journey and
to know that the fruits may be born in later harvests.
And, with the forces around me, I release this with
love, faith, and trust and say,
So be it.
And so it is.

Let the candles burn as long as you like.
Cut the apple into slices and leave a slice next to the flowers
for a day or two. Eat and share the rest with those you love
as a symbol of sharing the harvest.

*To be performed on the evening of the autumnal equinox.

Spell for Halloween (October 31)

After sunset,
light a white candle or a candle made of natural beeswax.
Place a pumpkin, gourd, or squash next to the candle.
Have a glass of apple cider at hand.

Say aloud:
*On this turning point in autumn,
time bends toward the great shadow.
As the darkness closes upon us each day,
so do the realms come closer to our lives.
I acknowledge the spirits in the realms around us
and ask that they be blessed and loved,
that they receive healing and light.
I remember and send love to those beings
from my life who are no longer here on this earth,
and I ask that they guide and bless my
work and life and the lives of those around me.
On this evening of magic and closeness,
I offer my respect and memory to those
who came before me. Ancestors, prophets,
saints, and ordinary ones:
You are remembered.
For the greater good of all, I say,
So be it.
And so it is.*

Raise your glass to the memory of loved ones.
Let the candle burn as long as you like.

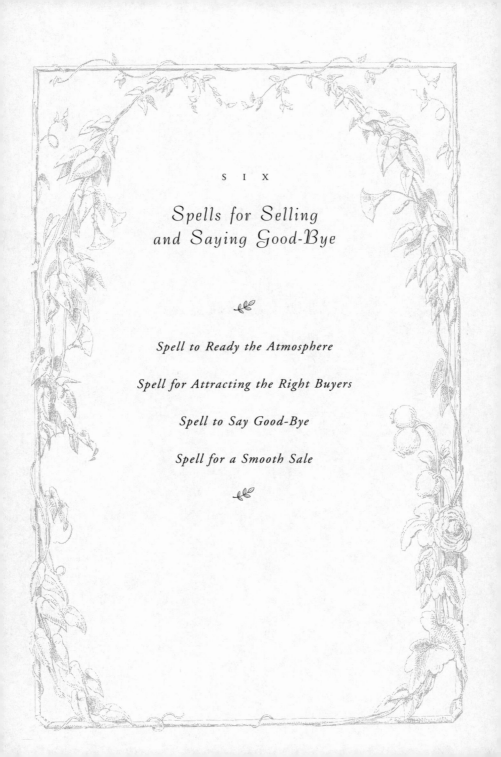

Spells for Selling and Saying Good-Bye

Spell to Ready the Atmosphere

Spell for Attracting the Right Buyers

Spell to Say Good-Bye

Spell for a Smooth Sale

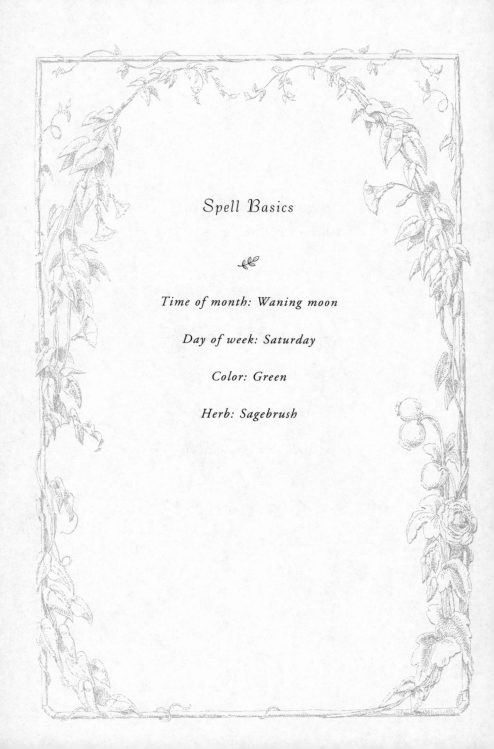

Spell Basics

❦

Time of month: Waning moon

Day of week: Saturday

Color: Green

Herb: Sagebrush

One of the hardest things we have to do in life is let go of a home, particularly a childhood home or a house you've lived in with your family for a significant amount of time. Your house is a silent member of your family, always there when you need it, occasionally demanding some attention, but invariably a place in which you rest, recharge, and find yourself again. Saying good-bye to this isn't easy. Even if you're looking forward to moving into your dream home, or downsizing for a simpler, more mobile life, you may find that you're melancholy about the transition. It's normal; you're ending a friendship.

Because of the emotional charge your home can take on while you live there and the complex feelings you're bound to have when letting it go, selling your house can be a difficult experience. Not only are you giving up its very special security and atmosphere, but you're letting someone else have it. Giving a stranger your home is hard. Even though my family hasn't lived in our "growing up" home or hometown for at least ten years, we still drive past that house and pause, thinking back to the old days and wondering what the people who moved in are like. There can be a strong magnetic pull around a place when it isn't "let go" consciously.

These "sticky" emotions can impair your ability to sell your house and make that letting-go point painful. Performing a few simple spells along the way can ease the transition and make the good-bye less stressful.

PREPARING YOUR HOME FOR THE SALE

I can't resist stating the obvious: Clean your house. Not only does your home have to be clean enough to attract a buyer, but it needs to be clear of any psychic energy that might inhibit interested parties. Sure, you don't want dust bunnies flying in their faces or streaks on your windowpanes lit up by the sun, but you also don't want your anxiety or fear lurking in your atmosphere, darkening deal-minded visitors.

Look at what you might be feeling. Your emotions may not be all nostalgic and warm—they could be mixed with some negativity you don't even notice. For instance, you might fear never finding a buyer, in which case you could become overeager and put off interested parties. Or you might be harboring some fear of disaster—that your furnace will break down, for instance, the house's foundation might not pass inspection. There's always phantom worry, too, like "What if the title search is a problem?" or "What if the lawyers or inspectors have issues?" These negative thought patterns and emotions permeate the atmosphere and make the house less receptive to potential buyers. There's truth to the notion of "smelling fear" in the air.

Once you've got your house together physically and you're ready to show it to prospective buyers, cast the spell for clearing the atmosphere. I know real-estate brokers who carry their own sagebrush sticks to clear properties before showing them, and there's a reason why: It works.

SECRETS FOR SMOOTH SELLING

Once you've cleared your house, you begin the selling phase. Much like dating to find the right marital partner, finding the right buyer can take time and patience. If the real-estate market is tight, sellers enjoy many prospects and often don't have to try too hard. However, when the market is so-so or glutted with properties, it can be hard to find even remote interest in buyers. I've heard of people doing all sorts of things to sell their homes, including burying a statue of Saint Joseph upside down in the yard (I hear this works, but what if you don't have a yard?), but I myself rely on spells—there's less work required.

As in dating, when looking for a buyer it's best not to be too eager or too standoffish or too quickly dismissive. My client Emily had a dream piece of real estate, one that "everyone" said would sell overnight. Emily got a bit cocky because she knew her home was in a desirable neighborhood and had the right number of rooms, appliances, and luxuries that "everyone" wants. Without thinking too much about it, she handed an exclusive listing over to a real-estate partnership that specialized in her neighborhood (where "everyone" goes when they're selling a house) rather than going with a broker who was a friend but did not specialize in that location. Her chosen brokers listed Emily's place at 10 percent over market value—what "everyone" does—and received one offer right away, which fell through. After the price was adjusted slightly to attract more prospects, another offer came in, and this one fell through, too. It was at this point that Emily came to me, having yanked her property off the market in disgust. Three months had elapsed since her supposed "overnight" deal was meant to happen, and now that it was summer, the selling season dwindled.

I asked Emily what kind of buyer she was trying to attract, and after a glib "Anyone who can come up with the money," she admitted that she hadn't given it any thought.

Having lived in her home for a good fifteen years, Emily had sunk much of her heart and soul into its improvements, yet she was trying to unsentimentally unload the property. When I pointed this out, Emily was slightly embarrassed; she hadn't considered her home part of her "family," but realized it was important to her that its new owners were "good people." When I asked her what she thought of the brokers, she recognized that she didn't really care for them as people but had previously felt they would come up with the best deal. After reconsidering, she contacted her friend and suggested that she (the friend) and the brokers from the partnership work together and split the commission. Emily performed some simple spells when it was time to put the place back on the market in the autumn, and it sold within two weeks—at a price above its listing price, and after dueling bids from clients of each of the brokers.

While it's hard to pinpoint just why Emily's real-estate transactions didn't go smoothly, I can suggest a few undercurrents of "anti-sale" energy. In dating terms, Emily was just trying to land a rich partner, giving no thought to compatibility or appropriateness. This is insulting to Vesta, the strong and self-reliant goddess of the hearth. After all, Vesta rules the very core of the home that Emily worked on and lived in for fifteen years—why should she play host to a new tenant without being asked? Vesta energy can keep people from taking root, even if they want to. Second, Emily didn't pay attention to any part of the selling process—she followed the crowd, doing what "everyone" was doing. In selling your home, your intuitive choices are far more important than the flow of the market or your neighbor's experience. Emily at first turned her back on Vesta and her instincts in favor of an effortless money-making deal. Once she put her energy in line with her intention and her instincts, the sale could happen.

When you decide it's time to sell your home, ask Vesta to help, and be sure to pay attention to the transaction. Especially when market conditions are adverse, you'll need to stay as open to magic as possible.

The excitement of negotiating the deal is over—you've sold your house and you're reasonably secure that the final transaction will be done and your movers will show up on time. Now what? You may have normal moving jitters as you go through your things and pack up, remembering tiny details that must be done before that final day. You'll be very busy—and very likely to overlook saying good-bye.

And yet just as in love relationships where it's normal to part and say good-bye, moving away from your home, your garden, your neighborhood is worthy of a real ritual. My family still hasn't gotten over leaving our childhood home, and I think part of the reason is that we never really said good-bye. Those nostalgic feelings and longings for the home you left behind can hinder your ability to set up and enjoy your new home. It's like bringing old baggage into a new relationship—eventually it takes a toll.

With spells, there is a very specific way of saying good-bye, and one in which you can be sure you won't drag baggage along with you. Saying good-bye is about withdrawing your energy from your house, room by room, even memory by memory. The longer you've lived in a house, the more you've woven your energy there, and you need to collect it so you can move on.

The last time I moved, I waited until after the movers had left and looked over the rooms where I'd lived for eight years. So much had happened in that time—I'd left advertising and started writing books and consulting, I'd met my husband, married and had a baby. I'd given one of my friends a huge fortieth birthday party and cooked my first Thanksgiving dinner. So many memories came to me as I wandered around those empty rooms. Aloud, I thanked that apartment for being such an important and supportive space, closed the door, and didn't look back.

My client Natasha came to me just after she and her husband had moved to a new city. Being a bright, hard-working career woman and mother of two, Natasha didn't put much time into being introspective or ritualistic. The change had been rough on her family, with her husband living in the new city months before they actually moved. When it came time to physically settle in her new home, Natasha was relieved that the family was together again. Months after arriving, though, she still felt uneasy in her new house. Some rooms still needed finishing touches like curtains or carpets, and since the house was considerably bigger than their previous one, some rooms were very sparsely furnished. Usually a project of this sort would have interested Natasha— she took pleasure in choosing fabrics and styles, and seeing her ideas come to life. But she was listless and didn't care for her house. The children left their toys out and beds went unmade because she couldn't find the energy or the heart to care much.

When Natasha finished describing her experience to me, I asked her one question: "How did you say good-bye to your last house and city before you moved?"

She didn't have an answer, since she hadn't said good-bye. She admitted that she longed for the old house, the familiar town, and the quirks and atmospheres that made her feel at home.

In meditation, I had her go back to that house, room by room, and withdraw her energy, saying good-bye to the place. When, in her mind's eye, she got to the room where her children's growth was marked inside the closet door, she began to cry. Her babies were born in that house; the garden she planted over the years was no longer hers. Natasha had to say good-bye and let go of the attachment to these powerful, heart-filled places.

After our session, Natasha went home feeling sad, but it took only a day or two before her mood shifted and the gusto for decoration and being really "at home" in her new house took over. Her children teased her about her zeal for making their home complete, but she wisely involved them in choosing some elements so that they all felt totally settled and happy.

Saying good-bye may seem unnecessary, and in some cases you may just want to say "Good riddance." Yet as a rule you can only benefit by giving yourself a chance to collect your energy, be mindful of the past, and ask that the change you are making be blessed. Closure is very healing and also allows the cycle to start over once again.

Spell to Ready the Atmosphere

On a Saturday during a waning moon
and in the second hour after sunset,
light a white candle.
Place a glass of water and
a sagebrush stick next to the candle.

Say aloud:
With Vesta's blessing I call in the
forces of the elements, spirit, god, and goddess
to join with me in purifying this home
and readying it for those who may live and thrive
here next.
With this smoke I release this house from our
roots, our emotions, our life force,
and with this water I cleanse this space
and prepare it to support others.

Light the sagebrush. Carry it from room to room,
allowing its smoke to linger.
Carry the glass of water into each room and
sprinkle some from your fingertips.

Say aloud:
This house is now ready to shelter
and protect, for the greater good of all.
So be it.
And so it is.

Blow out the candle. Empty the remaining water into a
plant or into your garden. Take the sagebrush stick with you
to ready your next home.

Spell for Attracting the Right Buyers

On a Friday during a waxing moon
and in the second hour after sunset,
light a pink candle and a green candle.*
Place some pink flowers in a vase with water.

Say aloud:
*I ask for Vesta's blessing
and for the cosmos to lend its gentle hand
in sending me the right buyers for this property.
I release my control and fear around making this sale.
On this day of Venus power I ask that people
of right hearts and minds find connection to this space
and that these walls will be filled again with love,
life, and connection to mystery and miracle.
I trust in this process and affirm that I
receive the right price in the right time.
For the greater good, I say,
So be it.
And so it is.*

If possible, light the candles when prospects come to
see your house. Refresh flowers in the vase as needed,
keeping fresh flowers in the house during the selling period.

*This green candle can be used in other
selling-related spells, too.

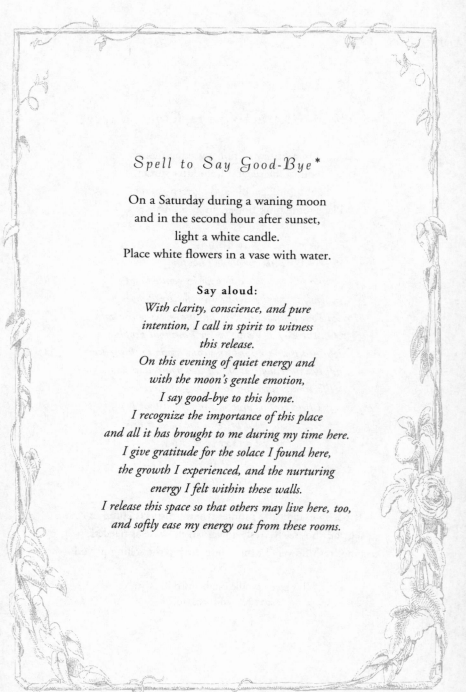

Spell to Say Good-Bye*

On a Saturday during a waning moon
and in the second hour after sunset,
light a white candle.
Place white flowers in a vase with water.

Say aloud:
*With clarity, conscience, and pure
intention, I call in spirit to witness
this release.
On this evening of quiet energy and
with the moon's gentle emotion,
I say good-bye to this home.
I recognize the importance of this place
and all it has brought to me during my time here.
I give gratitude for the solace I found here,
the growth I experienced, and the nurturing
energy I felt within these walls.
I release this space so that others may live here, too,
and softly ease my energy out from these rooms.*

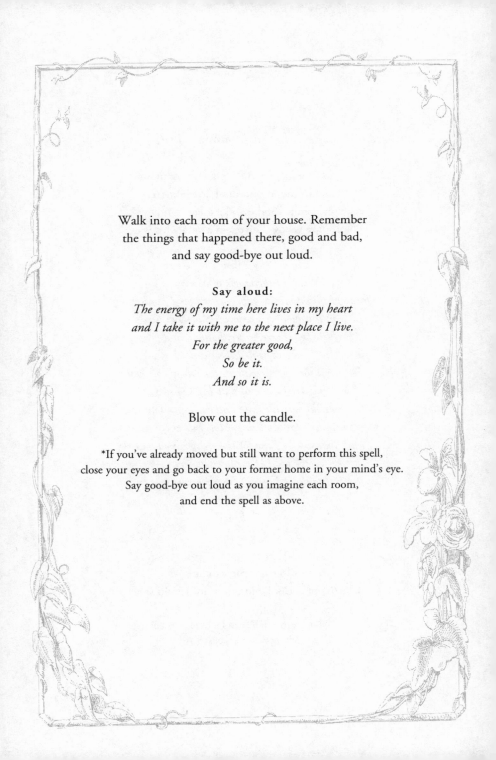

Walk into each room of your house. Remember
the things that happened there, good and bad,
and say good-bye out loud.

Say aloud:
The energy of my time here lives in my heart
and I take it with me to the next place I live.
For the greater good,
So be it.
And so it is.

Blow out the candle.

*If you've already moved but still want to perform this spell,
close your eyes and go back to your former home in your mind's eye.
Say good-bye out loud as you imagine each room,
and end the spell as above.

Spell for a Smooth Sale

On a Wednesday during a waxing moon
and in the second hour after sunset,
light a blue candle and a green candle.*
Place some yellow flowers in a vase with water.

Say aloud:
*I call in the magic of Mercury
for clear communications, contracts, and connections
in this hour of Venus, who bestows her
blessings of ease, grace, bounty, and joy
during this selling time.
I affirm that I participate in the sale of this home
in pure faith and that I relinquish
my hold over the land and my control over
the process for the best possible sale experience.
I ask that this be done for the greater good and for
the good of the new owners.
With faith and respect for the power of spirit
I say,
So be it.
And so it is.*

Blow out the candles.
Use the blue candle in other household spells.

*This green candle can be used in other
selling-related spells, too.

Afterword

$\mathcal{E}$xploring the magic of your hearth and home is one of the greatest pleasures of life. If you practice some of these easy rituals and pay attention to things you bring into your home and live with every day, your personal sense of security and satisfaction will be sizably increased.

While our lives are littered with distractions and diversions, timetables, deadlines, and due dates, we are still accountable for the time we spend with our families, with our friends, and with ourselves. Your home is one of the few places where you can exert your power and influence and have it benefit yourself and others. Honoring Vesta and her symbolic influence in your home life can help you create a true sanctuary—better than any decorator or housekeeper could.

Once you recognize your power to influence and create your home world, you'll never forget it. Have fun with your magic, and conjure a home blessed with the spirit of health, joy, and vitality.

If you have questions or want to share your experiences, contact the author at Execmystic@aol.com.

Index

Accidents, 44
air element, 22, 23, 80–81
air freshener, 85
air signs, 87
    mood shifting for, 97
allowing, 28–29
anchoring, 62
animals, 58
appliances, 85
artwork, 57, 59–60
astrological mood antidotes, 86–88
    for air signs, 97
    for earth signs, 96
    for fire signs, 95
    for water signs, 98
atmospheres, 30, 55
    elements and, 79–83
    mood and, 85–86
    spells for enhancing, 77–98
autumnal equinox, 142
    spell for, 151–52

Baby's room, 29, 61–62
    welcoming spell for,
        72–73

beams, 59
bedroom, 69
belief, 26–27
Beltane, 140
blessing and maintaining your home,
        spell for, 50
books, 57
burglaries, 43

Calendar year, nature and,
        138–43
camaraderie and ease, spell for,
        67
Candlemas, 139
    spell for, 145
changes in the home, 44–46
    spell for changing your home: trust,
        52
children's rooms, 70–71
Christmas, 104–6
    "hangovers" from, 113–14
    parties, 105–6
    spell to rekindle spirit of,
        116
clearing process, 39

computers, 58–59, 84–85
coziness, spell for, 90

*D*ays and hours, planetary, 33–34
dead rooms, 20, 60
dining room, 67
domestic help, 63, 64–65
   spell for commitment and honesty
      with, 75

*E*arth element, 22–23, 80, 88–89
earth signs, 87
   mood shifting for, 96
ease and camaraderie, spell for, 67
Easter, 108–9, 140
   spell for, 119
elements, 22–24, 79–83
   air, 22, 23, 80–81, 89
   astrological signs and, 87; *see also*
      astrological mood antidotes
   earth, 22–23, 80, 88–89
   fire, 22, 23, 79–80, 88
   symbols of, 88–89
   water, 22, 23, 81, 89
energy, 19–20, 38, 39, 60
   general spell for holding, 66
   grounding of, 61–62
   and moving into a new home, 41–42
   and things within rooms, 55–60

*F*amily room, 68
Father's Day, 110–11
   spell for, 123
feng shui, 21
fibers, natural, 57
figurines, 59
fire element, 22, 23, 79–80, 88

fire signs, 87
   mood shifting for, 95
flowers, 59, 133–34
funerals, 111–13

*G*ardens, 130–43
   indoor, 137
   outdoor, 136–37
ghosts, 40–41
good-bye, saying, 161–63
   spell for, 166–67
grandparents, 63, 64–65
   spell for health and joy for, 74
grounding, 61–62

*H*alloween, 142–43
   spell for, 153
Hanukkah, 106
   spell for, 117
hauntings, 40–41
healing, spell for, 92
healing atmosphere, for sad occasions,
   112–13
hearth, 23
herbs, properties of, 134–35
holidays and special occasions, 99–125
   Christmas, *see* Christmas
   Easter, 108–9, 119, 140
   Father's Day, 110–11, 123
   Halloween, 142–43, 153
   "hangovers" from, 113–14, 125
   Hanukkah, 106, 117
   Kwanzaa, 107
   Mother's Day, 110–11
   natural time points, 138–43
   New Year's Eve, 107–8, 118
   Passover, 108–9, 119, 140

reunions, 111, 124
sad occasions, 111–13
St. Valentine's Day, 110, 121
successful, spell for, 115
Thanksgiving, 109–10, 120
home
construction of, 37
energy of, *see* energy
life and personality of, 37–38
hours and days, planetary, 33–34
housecleaning, 46–47
psychic, 38–41
psychic, spell for, 48
and selling home, 158

*I*ngredients, 30–31
intention, 27–28

*K*ids' rooms, 70–71
Kwanzaa, 107

*L*ammas, 141–42
spell for, 150
lamps, 57
liveliness, spell for, 91
love and nurturing, spell for, 70–71

*M*agic, 21–22
elemental, *see* elements
objectivity and, 25–26
see also spells
maintenance, 46–47
spell for blessing and maintaining
your home, 50
May Day, 140–41
spell for, 148
mementos, personal, 57

memorial services, 111–13
metals, 57–58
mirrors, 57
molding, 59
moods, 85–86
moods, bad, astrological antidotes for,
86–88
for air signs, 97
for earth signs, 96
for fire signs, 95
for water signs, 98
moon, 32–33
Mother's Day, 110–11
spell for, 122
moving into a new home, 41–42
spell for, 49
music, 59

*N*ature, 58, 127–53
see also plants
new-baby room, 29, 61–62
welcoming spell for, 72–73
new home, moving into, 41–42
spell for, 49
New Year's Eve, 107–8
spell to welcome the new year, 118
night, 31–32
nurturing and love, spell for, 71–71
nylon, 59

*O*bjectivity, and magic, 25–26
outcomes, 25–26, 27

*P*assover, 108–9, 140
spell for, 119
phones, 84
photos, family, 57

planetary hours and days, 33–34
plants, 57, 59
   gardens, 130–43
   properties of, 134–35
plastic, 59
playfulness, spell for, 68
poltergeists, 40–41
protection, spiritual, 43–44
psychic housecleaning, 38–41
   spell for, 48

Renovations, 44–46
reunions, 111
   spell for, 124

Sacred space, spell for, 69
sad occasions, 111–13
safety and security, 42–43
   spell for, 51
sage, 39
St. Valentine's Day, 110
   spell for, 121
selling your house and saying good-bye,
   155–68
   secrets for smooth selling, 158–60
   spell for a smooth sale, 168
   spell for attracting the right buyers,
     165
   spell to ready the atmosphere, 164
   spell to say good-bye, 166–67
silk flowers, 59
smudging, 39
special occasions, see holidays and special
   occasions
spells
   for attracting the right buyers, 165
   for autumnal equinox, 151–52

for blessing and maintaining your
   home, 50
for Candlemas, 145
for changing your home, 52
for commitment and honesty with
   domestic help, 75
for coziness, 90
for ease and camaraderie (dining
   room), 67
for easing tension, 93
for Easter, 119
emotional components of, 25–26
for every room, 53–75
for Father's Day, 123
general atmosphere enhancers, 77–98
for Halloween, 153
for Hanukkah, 117
for healing, 92
for health and joy for grandparents,
   74
for holding energy, 66
for holidays and special occasions,
   99–125
how they work, 25, 34
ingredients for, 30–31
for Lammas, 150
for liveliness, 91
for May Day, 148
for Mother's Day, 122
for moving in, 49
for nurturing and love (kids' rooms),
   70–71
outcomes and, 25–26, 27
for Passover, 119
for playfulness (family room), 68
primary and supporting, 29–30
for psychic housecleaning, 48

to ready the atmosphere for selling,
164
to rekindle Christmas spirit, 116
to relieve a holiday hangover, 125
requirements for, 26–29
for reunions, 124
for sacred space (bedroom), 69
for safety and security, 51
for St. Valentine's Day, 121
to say good-bye, 166–67
for selling and saying good-bye,
155–68
for smooth sale, 168
for studying, 94
for successful holidays, 115
for summer solstice, 149
for Thanksgiving, 120
time and, 28–29
timing of, 31–34
for vernal (spring) equinox, 146–47
to welcome the new year, 118
for welcoming (new-baby room),
72–73
what they are, 22, 24–25
for winter solstice, 144
see also atmospheres; magic
spiritual protection, 43–44
spring equinox, 140
spell for, 146–47
stereo equipment, 59

studying, spell for, 94
summer solstice, 141
spell for, 149

Telephones, 84
televisions, 58–59, 84
tension, spell for easing, 93
Thanksgiving, 108–10
spell for, 120
time, 28–29
timing of spells, 31–34
trees, 131–33
trust, 28, 29
spell for changing your home,
52

Valentine's Day, 110
spell for, 121
vernal equinox, 140
spell for, 146–47
Vesta, 24, 106, 114, 160

Water element, 22, 23, 81, 89
water signs, 87
mood shiftings for, 98
willfulness, 27–28
windows, 58
winter solstice, 138–39
spell for, 144
wood veneer, 59